FUR
WITH AN
ATTITUDE

The Story of East Tennessee's
Elizabeth Grace

Jan-Carol
Publishing, Inc

"every story needs a book"

Fur with an Attitude
The Story of East Tennessee's Elizabeth Grace

Susan M. Howell

Published June 2015
Little Creek Books
Imprint of Jan-Carol Publishing, Inc
Copyright © Susan Howell
Design: Tara Sizemore

ISBN: 978-1-939289-60-5
Library of Congress Control Number: 2015940803

You may contact the publisher at:
Jan-Carol Publishing, Inc
PO Box 701
Johnson City, TN 37605
publisher@jancarolpublishing.com
jancarolpublishing.com

Carole,

Blessing + great grace
to you.
    In His great love
        Susan

This book is dedicated to the glory of God
and the building of His Kingdom.

Author's Note

Beloved one,

It has long been my joy to share Elizabeth Grace Howell (Gracie) with those whose lives have intersected mine. Welcome to our world.

I first saw her when she was just three weeks old. Little did I realize that our home was soon to be full of grace. Our lives were forever changed by this tiny brindle puppy so full of life, spunk, and, quite frankly, full of herself. She would challenge my patience, nerves, training abilities and sanity. We often wondered who had died and left her as queen.

Pastor Slagle once preached, "I need more grace at my house." I quickly replied, "When can I bring her and how long can she stay?" Today, I count it all joy to share Gracie with you through the written word. May she lighten your load and bring sunshine into your life.

Gracie's "mom,"
Susan

Acknowledgements

With Thanksgiving and Remembrance

I would like to honor and remember four very special sets of parents and my family who invested much in my life. Their love, patience and support have framed my personality and life choices.

My parents, Harold and Margery Miles whose love produced, raised, guided, instructed and tolerated me for eighteen years on the home front. Their love continued when I "grew up" after graduating from high school and moved to East Tennessee. I had far too few years with them as an adult. Mom passed away at age 48 and Pop was just 59. I was independent and stubborn and I'm sure I was a real challenge. This was magnified because my older sister, Cindy, was such a perfect child. She set the bar so high that I didn't even try to hurdle it. I carved my way as an athlete, tree climber and little stinker. Cindy, too, passed at an early age. She was just 43 years old when she left this life. Baby brother, Jonathan Scott, was stillborn and I did not get to see him. I miss them all and look forward to seeing them when my time comes. I am blessed to have my younger sister, Jennifer, close by. She lost our Mom when she was just seven years old and Pop when she was fourteen. We welcomed her into our home and lives at that point. We are very proud of the positive ways she has responded to the challenges and losses in her life.

Larry's parents, Fred and Evelyn Howell, accepted me as their own in 1968 when I became Mrs. Larry Howell. My time with my father-in-law was short, as he passed away soon after Larry graduated from college.

He was a kind and gentle man who served others and his Lord. Evelyn taught me how to cook and because of her I developed an interest in sewing. This skill later became a source of joy and income for me as I produced crafts and sold them at local craft shows. I cannot thank them enough for the encouragement and support they were to us as a young couple. Times were hard, money was scarce and study was the main focus while Larry earned his college degree. We lost Evelyn to cancer about twenty years ago and still miss her.

My Aunt Dorothie and Uncle Don played a big role in my development, too. What fun we had camping, snow skiing, producing musicals, driving to Colorado and swimming. They encouraged my spirit of adventure and assisted me in becoming the "pleasure seeker" I am today. They were always there for me, especially in the hard times.

As adults, Larry and I asked my best friend Carla's parents, if they would "adopt" us. They were more than glad to welcome us into their family. Fortunately for them, they did not have to raise me. Carl and Eva Hoffman set a beautiful example to us of love, giving and encouragement as they cheered us on in life. Chief and Ma ma', as we called them, never forgot a birthday or anniversary. Actually, I suspect that this was Ma ma's diligence and thoughtfulness. I still have the last birthday card they sent to Gracie and many sent to us.

Finally, I want to thank my husband, Larry. *Fur with an Attitude* is a picture of his love for me. We had just suffered the loss of our beloved boxer, Heidi. Larry was nowhere near ready to embrace a new puppy, yet he knew the addition to our family would help me cope with the loss. Because of his love for me, Elizabeth Grace entered our lives on October 11, 2005. How wonderful it is to have a great support team! It has been said that it takes a whole village to raise a child and I believe that is true. It may take more than a village to raise a boxer. It has also been said that I never truly "raise" my boxers as they never seem to grow up!

Special Thanks

My best friend Carla Forbes spent many hours helping me with this manuscript. She is an English major and kept my "i's" dotted and my "t's" crossed. She also knows what I meant to say instead of what I did say! That knowledge came in handy in doing the initial edit of this book.

Thank you for your assistance, encouragement and speaking the truth in love. You are the best!

Mike Britt and my husband Larry were my technical support. Everyone knows that I have the mechanical ability of a hamster and know just enough about computers to get myself into trouble. Larry was the "help desk" and Mike and Larry did all of the work cropping, scanning and arranging the photographs in the correct order. Thank you for your patience, and support!

Who's Who?

The names of many individuals are mentioned in this book. Permission was granted by the vast majority of people, however, a few could not be contacted, or asked that a fictitious name be used. All these folks were touched by the life of one very special dog, Elizabeth Grace.

Foreword

By Carla Forbes

It was one of those unforgettable moments. My daughter was choosing her wedding gown. I had called Susan to join us at the salon to share in our excitement. It seemed fitting that she be there since our families were intertwined in such a special way. Our husbands grew up together, and Susan had helped raise my two children during the years we were neighbors. That day marked a special decision for Susan, too. She had chosen a new boxer puppy, and she even brought along a photo so I could see what the puppy would look like. The dog calendar photo was for the month of October, and featured an adorable brindle boxer puppy. It was still September at the time, but soon, in October, her new puppy would be old enough to come home. I made the trip with her to bring "Gracie" home, and held that brindle ball of energy on my lap; unaware she would touch so many lives. As this story unfolds, Susan shares, often quite humorously, the challenges and joys of living with "Amazing Gracie."

In the Beginning

She was born above Roan Mountain State Park in a little East Tennessee hollow exactly two years ago today. I sometimes wonder just how far "above" she really did come from. I've even considered that another planet—Jupiter, Mars, or Pluto—may have been her place of origin. What about another galaxy? Or did she simply drop down from heaven just for us?

One thing I do know, she was destined to be ours. Gracie was shaped, formed, and brought forth for such a time as this. In her short season with us, she taught us so much.

Dogs Rule!

I was born into a family of cat lovers. My mother taught us the wonders of felines and she had absolutely no use for dogs. When I was a young child, I was bitten in the face by a dog. I do not remember the event, but a scar that divides my right eyebrow remains.

The physical scar has deepened with age, but the emotional scar has long since gone away. I can remember being afraid of every dog. The walk to school became a terrifying journey whenever a dog appeared.

Grandpa Warmann presented my family with our only dog. She was a blonde cocker spaniel named Taffy. Taffy and I bonded quickly. She was a wonderful baby to push in my doll stroller. Her gentle nature relieved and soothed my fear of dogs. Mom, however, was not impressed.

While we still had Taffy, I coaxed a dog to follow me home. Although I explained to Mom that the dog had just "taken up" with me, she would not let me keep it.

Taffy's days with us were short. She died with distemper and we were, again, solely a cat family.

Mom complained about the neighbors' dogs. She had no patience with the Ponces's German shepherd or the Jensen's "two stupid boxers." Aunt Dorothie and Uncle Don's collie, Missy, was big and intimidating to me. They kept her in the basement whenever we visited. With the exception of Taffy, I was still somewhat uneasy with dogs . . . until I met Tina.

Tina was half pit bull and half boxer. She had chosen my husband when he was twelve years old. As a puppy, Tina would stop eating and leave her food bowl to greet him. Who could resist that?

Tina was eight years old when Larry and I married. Her sweet nature and obedience won me over quickly. When our cat, Willie, jumped on the bed and bit me in the face twice in one morning, my loyalty switched from cats to dogs. Willie was our last cat. I never wanted another one after my experience with Willie. Standee, one of my childhood cats, spent her last years with us. She was over seventeen years old when she wandered off one day and found cat heaven.

Tina had been a wonderful companion for my husband. His parents worked and he was an only child. Tina became his best friend. I knew little about dogs and she made learning about dogs a joy. We spent many hours together while Larry was in college and worked.

Tina was extremely well-behaved. She always came when called, so we found it perplexing when she was gone most of the day and would not respond to our calls. She returned just before the thunderstorm. It took us a while to figure out that her excursion had been delightfully productive.

We awoke one rainy morning to find four tiny puppies in a sheltered hole that she had dug. I quickly moved Tina and her new family into the basement. Larry checked on them frequently. "How many puppies did Tina have?" he asked. I replied that there had been four. Upon hearing that, he said, "Well, there's five now!"

I repositioned myself to the maternity ward and watched in wonder as Tina gave birth to two more babies. I marveled that she knew exactly how to deliver, clean, and care for each one. When she cried to go outside, I watched as she went across the creek. I feared that she was delivering another puppy. A quick investigation proved me wrong. She knew exactly what she was doing. I stood amazed that God had given her such wisdom.

I named each of the pups. There were Sally, Chopper, Lucy, and Tigger. I cannot recall the other three names, as that was over forty years ago. We traveled a lot during this time, and as a result we did not get to know them as well as we got to know to our future dogs.

Ginger Dianna was our first purebred boxer. Ginger Dianna's name-sake, Dianna, was a dear friend who helped me find our puppy. Larry's mom, Evelyn, went with us to see the litter of five-week-old puppies. Evelyn expressed our feelings well when she said, "Those boxer puppies are the stuff." Each pup was fawn-colored, had a black mask, blue eyes, and a little, pointed head. Larry suggested we choose the most active female. This was a mistake we never repeated.

Ginger was an athlete. She was a hyperactive bundle of energy. Woe be unto whoever did not want to play with her. We spent hours a day playing with a tennis ball. The back porch became my workstation so I could accommodate the game. Rain, snow, wind, sleet, nothing would deter her from her fixation on her tennis ball. She filled our lives with love, joy, and exuberance.

After Ginger passed, we began our search for the next boxer. Thinking we were in the market for another fawn-colored boxer, we responded to an ad in the newspaper. The breeder had two litters, one fawn and the other brindle. The fawn litter was only about three weeks old. The brindle litter was ready to go. It was around this time that Larry said, "You know, those little brindle ones are kind of cute." He was right. A tiger-striped female caught my eye and heart. This time he made me choose.

We named her Gina Marie after Grandma Warmann. The veterinarian's staff nicknamed her "the tongue." They often teased that her tongue could reach from one exam room to the other. A gentle giant, her loving disposition won her many friends.

Mindy was a fawn-colored stray we adopted. She apparently had been used as a puppy factory. When she could no longer bear puppies, she was set out in an area called Stoney Creek. We found her at our local shelter. She shared our home with Ginger, and later with our new puppy, Gina Marie. We were privileged to have her in her later years.

Heidi Mareve was a gorgeous fawn-colored boxer. Her middle name was our own original creation—a combination of MAR for Margery, my mom's name, and EVE for Evelyn, Larry's mom's name. She was such a blessing to us for nine years.

Now we are totally hooked on boxers. They make us laugh every day. Their comical faces, goofy antics, and lovable dispositions make them irresistible! Having a boxer in the family is like having a resident clown. Everything is a game. Each boxer has been a four-legged entertainment center. They have shared such joy, loyalty, and love with us.

Boxers are known for their intelligence. Most seem to wind up inside the houses of their owners and many become bedfellows. I can't imagine a home without a boxer. They just seem to assimilate into our family. Each one that we have shared our lives with has been a unique creation and has blessed our lives.

The Hand of God

Never have I seen such evidence of the hand of God as I did in the circumstances surrounding our precious Heidi's passing. Our God is good all the time.

As our boxers have aged, I've prayed for the Lord to prepare my heart for the day that I lose them. Oh, that dogs would just live longer! Somewhere in His plan, He determined that their days would be much shorter than ours. Perhaps this is so that we may enjoy several dogs throughout our lifetime.

Heidi was diagnosed with boxer myopathy when she was seven years old. Someone recommended that we see the boxer heart specialists at Ohio State University, so we made a trip to OSU for a complete checkup. She was on medication to control her condition. We understood that she could die suddenly.

In May her rear leg gave way and she fell on our kitchen floor. She struggled to get up, but after that she was fine. Heidi had been through one knee surgery a couple of years before and now she needed surgery on the other knee.

With all of her other health concerns, we decided to postpone knee surgery and purchase a custom-made knee brace. She fell another time at our favorite walking trail. We thought her knee was giving out and causing the falls. The brace proved useless, as we could not keep it in place. About three weeks ago, she fell again on one of my big, beautiful pink flowers. During the last two weeks of her life, she panted when she went outside. We suspected that she had allergy problems, as she'd had additional symptoms.

One Sunday began as a normal day. Heidi let us sleep a little later, waking us up at 7:00 a.m. At 7:30 a.m. she was standing at the bottom of the steps, wagging her tail. She was ready to go to the walking trail, as we did every morning.

Heidi and I loaded up the car. I put yummies in the back seat with her. She usually gobbled them up immediately, but this morning she was not interested in eating. We arrived at the trail and parked at our usual spot. I opened the back hatch and I leaned her three-step stool against the back of the car. The stool made entering and exiting the car so much easier for her.

We headed for the loop section of the trail. There were two other pet owners on the trail and each was moving in a different direction. I debated which direction to go, as Heidi did not do well around other dogs.

To my left was a man who walked his aggressive black poodle daily. To my right I saw a man who I had seen for the first time yesterday. He was different. I remember he had curly hair and looked to be around fifty years old. He walked in a unique way with his small dog. I opted to go in the direction that intersected with him.

As we reached the trail, Heidi's back leg buckled and I helped her lie down. Her eyes became still as I spoke gently to her. I had already rehearsed in my mind what I would do if the end came in this way. Although I knew canine CPR, I determined that I would not administer it. I watched as her tongue became blue. She drew two final breaths as her life here ended.

My love for Heidi was what enabled me to let her go. She'd had a wonderful life and had been so happy that morning. She died doing what she loved to do. I was at her side and saw her through to the end. What a fitting and peaceful death. I would choose the same for myself or anyone that I love.

About this time the curly-haired man and his dog had reached the spot where I sat with Heidi. "Is there anything I can do?" he asked.

"I've just lost my baby," I replied.

"How can I help?" he replied.

"If you would help me put her in the car, I would appreciate it so much". He was more than glad to help.

I returned to the car to retrieve one of her blankets. We rolled her onto the cloth and together lifted her into my car. Heidi weighed eighty pounds and I could not have lifted her myself. I was so grateful for his help. His little companion sat quietly as we completed our mission. I thanked him for the kindness he had shown me in my moment of need. I cannot remember what he said, but we parted ways and I never saw him again.

In retrospect, I am fully convinced that he was an angel sent by Father God to help me that day. I remember his kindness, how different his appearance was, and the fact that I only saw him twice. I will always be thankful for his assistance.*

I called my friend Terrie and asked her to let my friends know that I would not be going to church with them that morning. I had not memorized their phone numbers and I really did not want to talk to anyone just then. Although I had woken Terrie up, she offered to come to the trail and help me with Heidi. I assured her that I was okay and that Larry and I would need time alone.

I was so shaken that when I backed into our driveway I let the clutch out while the car was still in gear and the engine was still running. The car jumped and the engine died. Larry knew something was wrong when I came inside. When I shared the shocking news, he was in disbelief. Every day it becomes more of a reality to us.

We left Heidi in the car and set about the grim task of digging her grave. Larry suggested we bury her next to Gina Marie, as they had shared several years together. The ground was parched and dry. We were forced to use an axe for the majority of the time that we were digging. Our house is on the edge of the woods, and as we dug, a beautiful deer appeared less than twenty feet away from us. She looked at us with big, gentle eyes as if to say she understood our pain and that we were not alone. Somehow, her presence assured me that the Lord was watching over us. The deer came three different times as we were crying, talking, and digging.

After we had finished, Larry went inside to put his contact lenses in. This gave me some time alone with Heidi. I sat on the back hatch of my car and draped myself over Heidi. I kissed her and stroked her soft fur. I remembered the Biblical story in which Elijah had laid his body over the body of a dead child and the child had come to life. I wept and wept over my loss. These words came from my heart and lips: "Thank you,

Lord, for the gift of Heidi. She has been such a blessing. All that I have is really Yours. I release her to You." As I spoke, I heard the sound of wings fluttering. Several mourning doves chattered and flew out of the woods. The most supernatural peace flooded my spirit. This peace has not left me since then. The Lord has truly carried me on His wings of grace and comfort. I have perfect peace concerning her passing. I can truly say that I know the meaning of the passage in Isaiah that says, "Surely He has borne our grief."

I will always be grateful to the Lord for choosing me to care for Heidi. We were so devoted to her. We had invested so much in her. Whatever we gave to her, she returned to us in abundance. She was a treasure and we were blessed to have shared our lives with Heidi.

From the workers at the Elizabethton High School who gave her treats every morning to officer Hardin who shared his peanut butter sandwich crusts, so many people loved our little Heidi. Among the people who loved her were preschoolers whom she dearly loved, her veterinarian, the University of Tennessee Veterinary School staff, the Ohio State University Veterinarian staff and students, our dear friends, and anyone Heidi met along her daily walks. How could you not love one who was so full of life and loved you so much?

Our lives were made richer because of Heidi. God has been so good to us. Heidi was our comedian. She made us laugh every day. She was my walking partner, a playmate, a faithful friend and companion, a joy, and one so full of life. It was a privilege to have shared nine-and-a-half years with her.

There will always be a place in my heart for Heidi, as there is for Lucy, Tigger, Ginger, Mindy, and Gina Marie. Each one was God's unique creation and they blessed us so abundantly. Life is truly a precious gift. Cherish and treasure all whom He has entrusted to your care.

I want to thank everyone who helped us care for Heidi. If you ever met her, you helped bring joy into her life. She dearly loved people.

As for me, I cannot imagine the Howell household without a boxer. I am quite sure that just as He directed us in choosing all of our previous pups, He has another one waiting.

"There is a time for every purpose under heaven."
Shalom

Written days after Heidi's death in July of 2005. Revised in May of 2011 and August of 2014.

*In July of 2011, I was telling my friend about the angel. Tears welled up in her eyes as she announced, "I've seen him. He looked exactly like the angel who had helped me."

She remembered well the day in 2000 when she and her three-year-old grandson were walking the trail. The sky was grey and strong winds quickly brought lightning and thunder. She hurried towards her car, but was unable to carry her crying grandson due to a back injury.

Suddenly she heard a gentleman's voice behind her say, "Let me carry him." He picked up the child. She instructed him to go ahead and not wait for her. Arriving at her vehicle, she noticed that there were no other cars in the parking lot. He placed her grandson in his car seat. She leaned over to buckle him in as her grandson kept looking past her in the direction of the gentleman. When she turned to thank him, he was gone. Her grandson explained it to her, saying, "Mam maw, he was an angel."

Not Just an Ordinary Day

It began as an ordinary day at the medical center where I worked when my coworker, Kim, brightened my day. Her brother-in-law had two female boxers and each had had a litter of puppies. Kim knew how much I loved boxers. There is absolutely nothing as cute as a boxer puppy. Their blue eyes and little pointed heads define adorable.

I was overjoyed as I thought about the puppies. I told Kim that I wanted to see them. I decided to wait until they were about three weeks old before I saw them. Their eyes would be open by then and I could get to know their personalities.

I explained to Kim that there was no way that I would be getting one of the pups. Our current boxer, Heidi, was growing older and had a severe heart condition. No matter how cute the puppies were, I would not even consider bringing one home. Heidi deserved better than that. . . . Never say never.

How many ordinary days wind up becoming extraordinary?

We're Off to See the Puppies

The three weeks passed quickly. Kim and I arranged to meet at a second-hand store in the Village of Roan Mountain. From there, I would follow her to where the puppies were. Kim's husband, Steve, as well as their children, Hayden and Jordyn, accompanied her. Steve's brother, Rich, owned the dogs.

The drive was beautiful. We passed Roan Mountain State Park and turned onto a county road. Approximately one mile further we pulled into Rich's driveway and were greeted by the adult dogs.

As I opened my car door, a beautiful fawn female boxer leaped over me and took her place on the passenger seat. Hello, Mama Molly! She was beyond friendly. Her exuberance and joy were incredible.

I climbed out of my vehicle and was greeted by Mama Penny, a lovely dark brindle boxer, and Daddy Brodie, who was also brindle. A large black dog also joined the welcoming committee.

Mama Molly remained in my car and had to be coaxed out. Although her puppies were just three weeks old, she seemed to have springs in her feet. With enthusiasm that is uniquely boxer, she danced in delight and leaped for joy. This was no ordinary dog.

Mama Penny and Daddy Brodie were calm and well behaved. Friendly and well-adjusted, they seemed glad to have company. Mama Molly was different. She was ecstatic that I had come. Rich began to share her story.

Molly was just eighteen months old. While this is not the ideal age to become a mother, it had just kind of happened. Molly had been a boisterous, rowdy pup who had become a neighborhood problem. When someone had threatened to shoot her, her original owners had given her to Steve's brother.

While Penny and Brodie knew about family planning, Brodie and Molly apparently knew about "young love." Penny gave birth to eight puppies on August 14. Only three survived. They were all dark brindle and looked very much alike.

Molly delivered seven puppies on August 22. Five of the pups survived. Having a fawn mother and brindle dad, the puppies included two fawn females, one fawn male, one brindle male, and one brindle female who would later be known as Amazing Gracie!

When I first visited, the litters were still separated. Each mom and litter had a doghouse and a pen. I enjoyed cuddling the little tykes and playing with them. I must say that I quickly fell in love with the runt in Molly's litter. She was fawn and had a lot of white on her face. Being the smallest, she loved to snuggle more than the other puppies in her litter. Oh so cute!

I must have stayed for at least two hours, and I thoroughly enjoyed myself the entire time. It was so good to see a new generation of boxers. However, I still had no intention of getting one.

What a difference twenty-four hours can make. The next morning Heidi died at the walking trail. I was quite upset when I called Rich that evening and told him about Heidi. After telling him, I added, "I'm too upset to talk right now, but I want one of those puppies."

"You'll have first pick of the two litters," was his reply.

The Power of Hope

Just knowing that one of the puppies was going to be mine brought such hope to my spirit. I marveled that the Lord had let me see them the day before Heidi's death. If ever there was a puppy hand-picked for me, it was the one that I chose from the two litters.

The next week, I went back to visit the pups. This time I found that they were all mixed together. Each mom was loose and the puppies were nursing from either mother. I didn't think anything of it then, but since then I've often wondered if this was the root of Gracie's problem with authority.

Each pup had a distinct personality and I was privileged to spend plenty of time with them in the coming weeks. I could watch them interact and develop. My original plan had been to purchase a brindle female. Heidi had been fawn and I knew it would be good to have a brindle one this time. I have never expected a new puppy to take the place of the previous one. I respected the fact that each pup was a unique creation. Each has been cherished for who they are.

I nicknamed Penny's litter of three "the three musketeers." Being eight days older, they pretty much stuck together. They were all a very dark brindle and I decided that I liked the lighter ones better. That eliminated three. The owners were keeping the fawn female with the solid black mask. Now we were down to four, two of which were boys.

I must say that the runt of Molly's litter was especially sweet. She was fawn and had a wide "skunk stripe" up her forehead. I looked forward to the evenings when I would make the drive to Roan Mountain and visit the puppies. They were always so glad to have company. I usually entered their pen and played with them until it was dusk.

I quickly learned that this was a litter of roughnecks. Their favorite activity was to engage in what I called "the growly bities." I have observed several litters of boxers and Molly's was, by far, the most rambunctious and rowdy. I began to notice that the little runt would go to a corner by herself and growl when the others approached her. I called my vet to ask about this behavior. She cautioned me that it was anti-social behavior and perhaps I should choose another pup. I later realized that this was the pup's way of defending herself against the other larger littermates. She probably turned out to be the sweetheart of the family!

One evening while playing with the puppies I remember thinking, "Do you really want one of these wild things?" I guess the thought did not stick.

Although I wanted a female, I noticed that the fawn-colored male was more laid back. I nicknamed him "Mr. Congeniality." He won my heart over. I called Rich that night to tell him that I was considering choosing Mr. Congeniality. "It's too late," he had said, "I had a couple come tonight and choose him. They will pick him up next week." I knew I wasn't sup-posed to get a male.

Meantime, back at the growly bitie ranch, the brindle female with the white skunk stripe on her forehead wormed her way into my heart. She was light brindle, had white stockings, and had a white band that went partially around her neck. She had more flash (white) on her coat than our previ-ous boxers. She was quite striking. She had a twin brother that looked so much like her that, until I got to know them, I would have to turn them belly up to determine which was which. I knew that she was going to be a handful. Strong spirited and stubborn, she would challenge my boxer-raising abilities. Those abilities have been questioned as our boxers never seem to grow up!

I dug out the little knit baby hat that says "Little Boxer" on it. I had bought it years ago at a yard sale and each of our baby boxers had had their picture taken while they were wearing it. I put it on her. She wasn't impressed, but she tolerated the initiation into the Howell family.

Her name was to be Elizabeth Grace. Elizabeth means, "consecrated to God." Her life motto is "live life to the fullest." Grace, of course, reminded me of the grace of God—His grace in preparing her for us and the grace we would need to raise her. She became known to us as Gracie. Every now and then we would call her Lizzie or Lizzie Grace.

Fashioned by the hand of the Father
And birthed August 22, 2005

Elizabeth "Gracie" Grace
Her name a continual reminder of God's grace

Has been adopted into the home and hearts of
Larry and Susan Howell on October 11, 2005
8 pounds 8 ounces as of October 12, 2005

"The Lord is gracious, loving and full of compassion."
Psalms 111:4

His Perfect Timing

When Gracie was six weeks old, I made the trip to Roan Mountain to visit her. It was raining this particular evening, so Rich had her and "Mr. Congeniality" in the house. I sat down on the floor to play with them. Of course, they were much more interested in wrestling and what we later named face wrestling.

There were three people sitting on the couch. Rich explained that they had come to pick up the male fawn puppy. As I continued to interact with the puppies I heard someone say, "Sue?" No one ever calls me Sue anymore, so I knew it had to be someone who had known me many years ago. Sitting on the couch was my friend, Angela. She and I had walked a fitness trail together some twenty years ago. We became friends, as she had a boxer named Bullet and I had Gina Marie. Her husband, Mike, and grown son, Matthew, had come to pick up their new puppy. Mr. Congeniality was to become Rocky.

How perfect was God's timing on this one! Had they not been there when I went to visit Gracie, I may never have known that they owned her brother. This connection later led to us becoming family.

Welcome Home!

Two of my friends accompanied me as we made the trip to bring Gracie home. She was now eight weeks old. Terrie and Carla took turns holding Gracie as I drove home. Wrapped in a new pink baby blanket, she cried for a short time and then settled down and went to sleep. What a joy to bring my new puppy home.

My life was about to change. Fortunately I had lots of experience raising boxers. However, this one was different. She would challenge my best efforts.

But today she was a sweet little sleeping puppy and I was thrilled to have her home. I gave her a bath, which she tolerated well. She shivered afterward, so I put a towel in the dryer to warm it up. Oh my, how she loved to cuddle in a warm softie. We repeated this after every bath when she was young. It didn't take her long to figure out that the warmth came from the dryer. If one warm softie was good, a whole dryer full of softies was even better! Whenever I had the dryer door open, she would climb in. This lasted until she finally outgrew the capacity load. There was simply nothing like a warm softie.

Gracie's first veterinary visit was October 12, 2005. She was eight weeks old and weighed eight pounds and eight ounces. Her first bedtime story was read to her by a neighborhood child, Heather, on October 14. Her first official spanking was on October 15 for biting. That sure didn't take long!

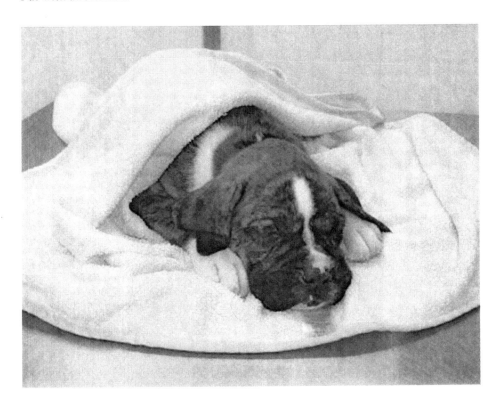

Doggie Daycare

I had actually done a lot of thinking about what I could do to make raising a puppy easier. Even before I brought her home, I decided that this puppy would be boarded on a regular basis so that she would be comfortable with us taking an occasional trip.

I visited Country Club Kennel to check out the facility. I met Regina, the owner, and took a tour of Doggie Daycare. I was impressed with the facility and Regina's love for animals.

Now Gracie was a handful as a puppy, especially on days when we both worked. One of us always came home to let her out at lunch, but by 5:00 p.m. she was ready to go. Wednesdays were different. Wednesday was the day she went to Country Club Kennel. She was about three-and-a-half months old when I loaded her wheelie backpack for the first visit. On my way to work, I dropped her off to spend the day with San, Regina's husband. She was thrilled to be there and never looked back as I got in the car and drove off. San took a special interest in her, and there were other dogs that she could play with. When I picked her up after church on Wednesday nights she was so tired. It was wonderful!

It was a welcome break in the middle of the week. San and Regina helped us greatly in raising her. Sometimes, when I had a day off, I would leave her there for several hours. What a blessing it was to have her tired when I returned. A tired boxer is a well-behaved boxer!

San would often welcome Gracie with the words:

Goodness Gracious!

The Shower

My dear friends at work surprised me with a puppy shower. The break room at my work area was all decorated in pink as we celebrated "It's a girl!" Charlene's granddaughter, Jessica, was there and she drew pictures of "Princess Gracie." They had no idea how much that blessed me. It was such fun to celebrate with my sister-friend, Cynthia, and some of my very best friends, including Tina, Terrie, and Maryann. I had never had a shower before. The presents meant a lot, but sharing in the joy of our new puppy meant even more. I shall never forget their kindness.

When Gracie was still a puppy my coworker, Cynthia H., added a Great Dane puppy, Maggie, to her family. We often shared puppy tales and laughed about the funny things our girls did. Being puppy moms together bonded Cynthia and I in a very special friendship.

Kindness is a beautiful thing. It costs nothing yet is priceless!

I should have known that we had a tiger by the tail!

Christmas Letter 2005

It's Christmas 2005 and time for the annual "Howell-o-gram."
As you may remember, Larry retired from the VA in October 2004. He had a short retirement, as in early 2005 he went back to work part-time doing contract work for the VA in Psychology Service. He is an outpatient therapist in the Post Traumatic Stress Program. He finds this work very fulfilling and he is able to make use of the graduate degree in clinical psychology he worked hard to earn several years ago.

Susan still loves her part-time position in breast care at Johnson City Medical Center. She still snow skis as often as possible, and in March of 2005 she went on a three-day trip to Snowshoe, West Virginia. She is a co-leader of a group of young worshippers called "Chosen Generation," through which she is privileged to teach the next generation expressive praise and worship.

2005 saw the fulfillment of two long-time dreams for Susan. One was a long bike ride on the Virginia Creeper Trail, and the other was getting a traditional German dress for this Christmas. Life after fifty was proving to be a time for fulfillment of dreams. . . .

In September our beloved boxer, Heidi, died suddenly. She had been diagnosed with a heart condition about two years previously, but had been doing well on medication. She was a very special little creature and she touched the lives and hearts of many people, who mourned her loss along with us. She will live forever in our hearts.

In October we brought home a boxer puppy we named Elizabeth Grace or "Gracie." She was eight weeks old and weighed eight lbs. and eight oz.

Her name was chosen carefully . . . "Elizabeth" means, "consecrated to God" and "Grace" reminds us of God's great grace. She is a brindle boxer with a white stripe on her forehead that Larry calls her "skunk stripe."

The culture shock of having a puppy is even more evident when you are over fifty! Our house often looks like "hurricane Gracie" has just passed through. Her best athletic event is the broad jump. She recently demonstrated the ability to jump five feet and land in Larry's lap (when this happened, he somehow managed to avoid spilling a cup of coffee he was holding).

Gracie is now in the "exploring" stage. Today we issued a "code Eve." For those who don't work in a hospital, "code Adam" is for a missing infant. Therefore "code Eve" is "where is Gracie?" When she disappears, you can be sure that mischief is in progress. You will never see the original of this letter because it has tooth marks in it.

Mattie and Me

Gracie quickly made herself at home as we worked through the adjustments of having a new puppy. A few days after we brought her home, she followed me to the mailbox. My neighbor, Jean, was driving down the road and stopped to ask where we had found Gracie. Jean was absolutely smitten and asked if there were any other pups left. I gave her Rich's phone number.

Mattie was the last puppy left from Penny and Brodie's litter. She was Gracie's half-sister, as Brodie had fathered both of them. Jean and her family made the trip to Roan Mountain and Mattie found a home with them. Although Mattie was eight days older than Gracie, she was smaller and as an adult weighed only about forty-five pounds.

Once Gracie recuperated from having ringworm on the top of her head, we were able to get the girls together. Mattie lived very close to us and at least once a day they romped, roughhoused, and played together. For anyone who has ever raised a boxer puppy, you know how important it is to get the "monkeys" run out of them.

What fun Mattie and Gracie had playing together. Chase and face wrestling were their favorite games. In the winter we would sled down the hill in the snow with the pups on board. One day I was building a snowman for William, our neighbor's son, who was confined to a wheelchair. Watching the production through a sliding glass door, William delighted in our snowman. Mattie and Gracie were not particularly helpful. Each time I would begin rolling a snowball, the girls would pounce on it and destroy it. To William's delight, I was finally able to complete a small snowman, no thanks to Gracie and Mattie.

On rainy days Mattie and Gracie would play inside the house. They chased each other in circles from my kitchen, through the dining room, and around the living room. I had to put a piece of carpet in the kitchen, as their feet slid out from under them when they made the turn in the kitchen.

After a long day at work, it was wonderful to have a neighborhood playmate for Gracie. Two boxer puppies can certainly be a handful, though. One day I posted this note on our door so our neighbor would know I had Mattie with me:

I have the two dogs.
Ransom: $25.00 for the small, dark one (Mattie)
Or will
Give you the small one back and $100.00
If you will take the big one.
Please answer soon.

Mattie's parents did come and get her, but they left Gracie with me. Imagine that!

When the pups were about five months old, we had to quit going to Mattie's house. They had discovered the cow pasture next door and what fun it was to smear manure on their necks. They also decided it was more fun to continue on their adventures rather than come when called.

Monkeybusters

Boxers are a very active breed. They simply must have their exercise, especially when they are young. We quickly developed a way to measure that need.

THE MONKEYS: "The monkeys" was a condition that Gracie developed when she required some exercise. If the monkeys could not be tended to quickly it accelerated into . . .

THE DOUBLE MONKEYS: During this phase the need for exercise was growing more critical. Gracie was beginning to act out, drawing attention to the fact that the double monkeys must be addressed.

THE GRAZILLAS: At this level we could expect foot tackling, body blocking, or boxer bolts, also known to us as "running trapezoids." Hard exercise became the priority. Gracie's brindle stripes and rowdy behavior earned her the nickname STRIPEZILLA or "the striped creature."

WE HAVE MET THE MONKEYS
AND THE MONKEYS ARE US!

FUR with an Attitude

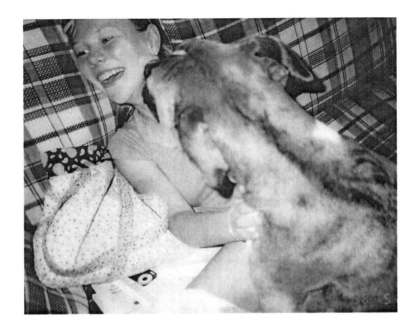

Our very first boxer, Ginger, had a pronounced cone-shaped bump on the top of her head. Being an attentive new puppy mom, I asked our veterinarian about the strange bump and was met with the response, "Haven't you ever heard of an intelligence bump?" Actually, I had not. Over the years I have found a correlation between the presence of the bump and how smart the boxer is. With Gracie we often wondered if hers was an auxiliary horn or a retractable spike.

Gracie had a pronounced intelligence bump, but she also had something I had never seen before. About one inch below the cone-shaped bump, her fur began to swirl as it came down her neck and back. We called it fur with an attitude. The fur actually stood up like a crew cut, made a white-tipped swirl to the right, continued down the center of her back, and produced a boxer mohawk of sorts. It ended at the area on her shoulders, covering about ten inches of her body.

The fur was a perfect expression of her high-spirited, spunky personality. It served as a constant reminder of her comical personality and kept me from taking her too seriously.

I understand that there is a breed of dog called a Rhodesian ridgeback. Perhaps somewhere, deep within Mama Molly's past, there was a ridgeback. Who knows? Perhaps it was just a special mark to help identify one so unique.

The "hairdo" is clearly seen in this photo of Gracie and Julia.

Third in Command

It isn't easy to be third in command, especially when there are only three in the household. It took months before Gracie finally gave up the role of "alpha dog." A dominant female never gives up easily. In her mind, she was born to rule, so what was OUR problem?

Larry's voice, stature, and firmness finally convinced Gracie that he was, in fact, the leader of our pack. Her bossy nature reared its head on occasion, but he always seemed to come out victorious.

Okay, so second in command isn't too bad. She chose to vie for that position. My voice, size, and firmness earned me nothing. Even my deepest, most firm voice yielded only a temporary submission, if anything. When she was several months old, I remember thinking, "This dog is never going to care if she pleases me or not."

Gracie had an authority issue. I often wondered if it was rooted in the fact that the two litters of puppies were allowed to nurse from both Molly and Penny. So, will the real mother please stand up? Regardless of how she developed it, I lived on the battlefield where this challenge played out.

Fortunately, I was not a novice when it came to raising a boxer. It has been said, however, that I never seem to get one raised. All of mine have been perennial children. Gracie's default mode was torqued. That fact, plus her dominant personality and confusion concerning authority, often frustrated my best efforts. She seemed to enjoy it when I raised my voice. If she could make me mad, we had a "fight" going on and she loved it! Obviously verbal correction was not my best weapon.

It was such behavior that earned her the nickname: Stripezilla!

The Tackle Box

If I could choose just one thing that I could have changed about Gracie, it would be the "back attack." She delighted in approaching me from behind and body blocking me. One fall afternoon I was attempting to rake leaves when she body slammed me from the rear. Running off gleefully, she was obviously delighted with herself.

Alright, this is it! "I'll show you," I thought. My plan was to discipline her just like a mother dog would. Immediately following the next attack, I ran her down, tackled her, and turned her belly up. Pinning her to the ground, I scolded her and then released my defeated foe. I felt a sense of accomplishment. I had forced her to submit.

Rising to her feet, she chased me down and body slammed me again. This was the best game ever. I had fallen right into her paws.

The popper gun was my most successful method of correction. This consisted of a small plastic gun that made a popping noise and shot confetti. It was a party favor that my friend, Matthew, had discovered at a local dollar store. Each gun could make six pops total. The noise was not that loud, but it served its purpose. In time, I only had to show her the device to achieve the necessary correction.

Unfortunately, the store quit carrying the popper guns and I was unable to find others. I tried a cap gun, but somehow that did not work as well. I would not carry it on our walks, as it looked like a real gun. Plus the noise was louder.

I'm sure that I made many mistakes as I worked with Gracie. I learned more things that did not work than things that did work.

Gracie had passed from the sweet puppy stage to what I call the juvenile delinquent era. It generally lasts from six months of age to two years. For Gracie, this was extended to four years. I frequently reminded myself of the scripture, "And it came to pass."

The Growly Bities

The growly bities are Gracie's version of a temper tantrum. They usually manifest when she does not get her way. She vented her frustration by grabbing my sleeve and growling. There is no harm intended, unless her teeth puncture my sleeve. If this does not work, she will attempt to tackle me.

All of my efforts to stop the behavior failed. If I yelled at her, her response seemed to be "You wanna fight? I'm up for it. Come on." My most successful method of controlling this has been to chase her with a mop, broom, or stick, which produces the trapeziodian run or a good old-fashioned boxer bolt. This seems to help her work off the frustration.

Simple things like changing the direction of our walk could set it off. Again, it was her strong, stubborn, defiant personality. She definitely thought of herself as the boss. I could sympathize with this as I, too, have a strong, determined personality. I like to call it being highly spirited. A boxer is of German origin and we are known for such behavior. I wanted to correct the growly bities without breaking her spirit and she challenged my best efforts.

The rules according to Gracie: Me, Me, Me. It's all about Me, Me, Me. Everything rotates around what I want.

The real rule: You are part of a family. It isn't all about you. We have a working relationship in which we give and take.

All of us eventually come to the realistic conclusion that it really isn't all about us. Gracie's will was so strong that I called her granite head. For almost four years she had the hardest head of any boxer I had raised.

Victory!

Today is Wednesday, April 13 of 2011. Gracie is five years and eight months old. I am rejoicing because I have just experienced my first real victory over the growly bities.

We started the day out right. It was about 8:00 a.m. when I pulled the car out of the driveway. Something didn't seem right about the vehicle. I pushed the clutch in to stop and retrieved the newspaper out of the box. As I attempted to change gears, I found that the shifter stuck in place. When I took my foot off the clutch, the pedal stayed depressed. I put my foot back on the clutch, turned the engine off, and sounded two long nasal beeps from my horn.

Larry came to the door in wonder. "There's something wrong with my car," I hollered. He took control by manually pulling the clutch up and backed the car down the driveway. A confused Gracie jumped out of the car. "What happened to my walk?" she seemed to ask. My CRV is the only "Gracie-proof" car we own. It's a rolling boxer mobile complete with special seat covers, leashes, collars, and fold-down seats. The interior usually has as much dog hair in it as Gracie has on her body.

Canceling our morning walk, I decided to make good use of my time by making some phone calls. I joined Gracie outside, completing the calls on a cordless phone while sitting on the back porch.

Gracie has never liked me talking on the phone. How could I possibly give my attention to some little appliance held to my ear when she's around? The whole situation was more than she could bear. We didn't get our walk and now I was on the phone. It was a perfect scenario for the growly bities.

Today I truly understood her frustration. When she started the growly bities, we went inside. Sitting on the steps, I called her to me. I asked her to sit down. Petting her, I gently explained that I truly did understand, but that I had done the best I could to take her for a walk. We simply could not go. Instead of staring me down, barking, and going into the growly bities, she turned her head in surrender and enjoyed the shower of affection. After a long hug and some cuddle time, she was content to surrender her will to mine.

Love surely does conquer a multitude of sins!

The Bobble

Boxer puppies have their tails docked when they are just a few days old. I used to think the procedure was cruel and unnecessary.

You must understand that boxers do not wag just their tails; they wiggle their entire rear ends. A boxer is excitement personified, especially when company arrives. If a boxer had a full-length tail, everything on the coffee table would be wiped out with the first "I'm home," my shins would probably be black and blue, and my knees would suffer from "tail abuse." Her tail would wipe out many decorative items, the walls would have tail marks on them, and small children visiting would have to wear protective eyewear.

A boxer's bobble will be anywhere from two inches to five inches. It depends on who docked the tail and what kind of mood they were in. Gracie has about a five-inch bobble. A young child in our neighborhood once asked, "Why don't he grow him a tail?" when he saw Ginger.

Gracie was spayed when she was eight months old. We have often said that she would not have made a good mother. She could never be still enough to nurse her babies, or even conceive them for that matter.

She is, however, an expert when it comes to docking tails. Every stuffed animal in our house has been properly "de-tailed" by Gracie. Occasionally, something is mistaken for a tail. The trunk of an elephant, for example, might be removed. Once the tail docking is completed, the victim is officially admitted into her family. It just seems to be the "mark" of being a boxer.

She's got the world by her bobble!

Tails, You Win!

Every so often Gracie will get a glimpse of what is left of her tail. When this happens, the chase is on. Round and round we go, where she stops, nobody knows. "It's too late, Gracie," we try to explain, "Someone has already beat you to it." Is it the fun of trying to catch her tail? Does she think someone is following her? Who knows what lurks inside that little striped head? Chasing her bobble is great fun until tiredness and/or dizziness ends the game and she settles down. All that energy spent on chasing something that isn't there!

We humans do the same thing. We catch sight of something or someone who will bring us excitement. We whizz right past what we DO have in pursuit of what is not meant to be ours. Maybe it was a part of our past, but it's not there anymore. We spend enormous time seeking after something that just isn't there.

Life, indeed, has its times and seasons. Spring, summer, fall, and winter. Each one offers a unique experience. Cherish each day as it comes. Release the past. Learn from the times and seasons of life.

Out of Reach

Having a puppy means you must rearrange your life for at least a time and season. A puppy explores everything with its mouth. So, if you don't want it destroyed or missing in action, don't leave it where the pup can get it. The trade-off is that you provide what is acceptable for the puppy to have.

There are many things in our household that are just for Gracie. Toys, chew bones, and her bedding are all things provided for her pleasure. There are also some things that she chooses to leave alone because they simply do not interest her.

There are also numerous things that she desperately wants and is not allowed to have. Take, for example, the shoes I just took off, my cell phone, my hand braces, leather ski gloves, and the bag of rawhide bully sticks. She is relentless in her pursuit of these items. She's a pleasure seeker. When she gets something on her mind, she simply does not forget about it.

The unreachables are kept on top of the refrigerator. We find this is the safest place and she usually forgets about whatever we put up there. We never have to wonder what Gracie wants. She is neither bashful nor shy. When she is hungry, she smacks her food bowl with her paw and cries. Should we fail to respond in a timely manner, the next step is to flip the bowl upside down. She has actually done a very good job training us!

Life's Fascinations

Her face in the stainless steel water bowl
(This caused such a stir that it had to be replaced with a crock type bowl)

Loose strings on the carpet

The reflection of her face on our black car

The toilet bowl

Rolls of toilet paper

Ever wonder why they call a family of puppies a litter?

FOR SALE OR LEASE

COULD YOU USE . . .

A YARD EXCAVATOR?

KITCHEN FLOOR CLEANER?
(Guaranteed no more crumbs on the floor
Complete with supersized tongue)

A BACK WARMER?
(Works best when placed between 2 humans
on a soft mattress)

A PATIENCE DEVELOPER?
(Constant entertainment—better than a 3-ring circus)

AN EXERCISE BUDDY?

A COMPANION?

A COUNTERTOP AND DISH CLEANER?
(Guaranteed to wipe clean all bowls
placed within her reach.)
Specializes in key lime yogurt and whipped cream

IT'S ALL YOURS WHEN YOU RENT/LEASE
"THE STRIPED CREATURE"

Just 50 lbs

Extra heavy-duty tongue

Large white feet

Optional "skunk stripe"

ALL FOR ONE LOW PRICE!
For a real deal call 542-0000 & ask for Susan.
For a GREAT deal call 542-4100 & ask for Larry.

Makin' Hair Fly

If you were to call my barber, Terry, at work and ask him what he is doing, he would probably reply, "Makin' hair fly." The hair may fly, but he is meticulous and gives a precision haircut every time. Ok, so one time he cut mine a little crooked. Once in thirty years is remarkable, though.

Not only is Terry a great barber, but he also loves dogs. He owns Jack, a Jack Russell that took up with him at his farm. Or should I say Jack owns him? Whatever, when Terry found out that we had a new puppy, he asked me to bring her with me to my next appointment. "Terry, you really want me to bring a boxer puppy to your shop?" I asked. He assured me that it would be alright and he would be careful about who he scheduled before and after me.

Gracie was thrilled to meet Terry. She thoroughly washed his face, neck, hands, and anything else she could get her tongue on. There were all kinds of new scents to explore and she loved this adventure. I kept a close eye on her as Terry cut my hair. Being the mom, I felt responsible for whatever she might plunder or destroy. Terry continued to assure me that she would be alright.

Although Terry had no other appointments scheduled, we did, unfortunately, have a visitor. The State Inspector just happened to come by that day. She was not exactly pleased with Gracie's presence at the shop. She reminded Terry that dogs were not allowed in the shop. The inspector then turned to me and asked if Gracie was a service dog. Surely you jest? A four-month-old boxer puppy as a service dog? Perhaps a comedian or clown act, but certainly not a service dog. I supposed she was trying to give us an out.

I could not truthfully tell her what I think she wanted to hear. Terry's shop is always clean, neat, and highly rated. This time we were BUSTED. There simply was no way out. We were like Bonnie and Clyde with a dog. Caught red-handed and red-pawed. Terry's rating was slightly reduced for a year, but no handcuffs or pawcuffs were needed and we served no prison time. We might have learned a lesson, though!

Wither Thou Goest

Dogs are pack animals. Larry and I were now Gracie's pack. They are also very social creatures. I have read that it actually stresses a dog to be left alone for more than eight hours.

This was no problem for me, as I generally loved to be with Gracie. She became my walking buddy. I also took her with me anywhere that dogs were allowed.

Returning from a walk one morning, I noticed that one of my neighbors, Bobbie, was having a yard sale. Gracie was still a big puppy, so I decided to drop her off at our home and then walk to Bobbie's house.

I was very pleased with my bargains and came home to show Larry. He was not as happy. "Don't you ever do that again," he told me.

"What are you talking about" I replied.

He didn't have to explain. The venetian blinds were torn down and lying on the couch. "She's been pitching a fit," Larry said. She had jumped up on the couch and tried to dig her way through the window. The blinds had been the victims.

From then on, Gracie went to yard sales with me!

Out of Town

By now, Gracie was used to her weekly trips to doggie day care. She loved going and I loved having a tired puppy at least one night of the week. The three-day trip we took without her was not quite as much fun. We gave this letter to San and Regina when we dropped Gracie off:

Congratulations!

You have been awarded custody of "the striped creature" for three days. I have no idea what you have done to deserve this, but remember the Scripture says, "And it came to pass."

You need to know:

1. She likes to sleep on the bed. Her choice is in the middle, with her head on the pillow. She will settle for the foot of the bed, in the middle. This is accomplished by placing her softie (blanket) on the spot you want her to lay on, patting the softie and saying repeatedly "this is Gracie's place." If this is unsuccessful, method "B" must be implemented. This method involves two strong people dragging her to the desired position.

2. She will eat most table scraps but is NOT allowed pork, bones, or chocolate. Her favorites are whipped cream out of a squirt can and meats.

3. When she hears you wake up, she will move up between the two of you and complete the "Gracie sandwich." You two are the bread; she is the filling.

4. Close the bathroom door tightly when taking a shower or you will have an "invader."
5. I have told her to mind her manners and NOT drink out of the toilet bowl, but I would not count on obedience.

Somehow, San and Regina survived the three-day stay. Although Gracie dearly loved them, she was glad to be home.

One Mother's day we sent this poem to Regina, as she was Gracie's "other mother":

I love to come and see your face
When I see Mommy pack my bag
Behind I surely will not lag.
For I will come your face to see
I jump for joy and wiggle with glee.
Together we have lots of fun
I play, we dance, and I love to run
You are my Mom when I'm away
And so I really have to say
I LOVE YOU!

Luv'em Lick em's

Regina also worked a stressful full-time job. One day she had had about all she could take at work. She arrived at home and went to the kennel to see Gracie. Normally, Gracie would have been bouncing and jumping, delighting in Regina's presence.

As Regina greeted Gracie, tears began to flow. Gracie sensed Regina's need and began to administer gentle luv'ems. Her long tongue washed Regina's face and dried her tears. As she gained momentum, the face washing turned into a facial massage. It so touched Regina that she wrote a poem called "Luv'em Lick em's." The poem was misplaced, but the love continued.

Gracie had brought sunshine into Regina's day and had blown all the clouds away. She was an expert at that. She seemed to have a sixth sense about her that allowed her to detect when someone especially needed her. I recall a walk we once took. As we intersected with an older man and his grown daughter, Gracie went right to the daughter to share some love. The lady told me, "You don't know how much I needed that. My dog just died and Gracie knew I needed love."

I sometimes called her "the day maker." Over and over again I would hear, "She's made my day." Dispensing love was one of her specialties. She had no prejudices and judged no one. She looked for people to whom she could deliver love. As we intersected with folks on our walks, she would stop to greet each one, fully expecting them to stop, too. A face like hers was hard to resist! Be it a person in a wheelchair, a toddler, a school-aged child, or just Joe Average, Gracie was on the spot to give her unconditional love.

There is nothing quite like the love of a dog!

The Buzzards

At the age of five or six months, each of our boxers, beginning with Gina Marie, has found the yard invaded by "the buzzards." The buzzards seem to come out of nowhere and take over.

Overnight these creatures set up their camp, which is marked with a boundary of flags. I introduced Gracie to these notorious villains. She found that as she approached the flags, her special collar made a buzzing noise. I taught her that when she heard this noise, she should run back in the direction of the house, away from the buzzards. Should she continue to move in the direction of the buzzards' camp, they would "bite" her on the neck. They always went for the neck. The discomfort was enough to get even Gracie's attention.

Gracie was a quick learner. Much as she did not like the buzzards, she respected their territory. I believe that Gracie thought they had abandoned camp when the flags gradually disappeared. She soon learned that her invisible enemy was still present. She also figured out that she could live on the edge of their camp and not suffer the consequences. I have watched her go to the edge of the boundary and listen to the buzzing. She knew that if she did not go any further, she was safe. The result of this tactic was that the battery in her collar was worn out.

One day I was inside the house and had left Gracie outside for just a few minutes. I looked toward the woods that adjoins our yard. "Oh, how cute, a little fawn," I thought. I soon realized that the "fawn" was Gracie! The battery in her collar was dead and she determined that she could explore just a little further. Always on the edge. That was our Gracie!

Healthy boundaries are a good thing!

Rocky Top

One Sunday we discovered a yellow jacket nest in the yard. Gracie never seemed to have learned to stay away from them. I remembered that her brother, Rocky, had a fenced yard and decided to call Rocky's mom, Angela to see if the "kids" could get together. This was the first of daily visits and began our adoption into the Britt family. Rocky looked like Mama Molly. He was a beautiful fawn boxer. Gracie favored daddy Brodie with her brindle stripes.

Angela, Mike, and their grown son, Matthew, had adopted Rocky when he was a wee little fellow, just six weeks old. He cried all the way home. He was a real cuddler and loved being held on laps. Rocky got off to a rough start. When he was about nine weeks old, Angela began to notice that he had lost hair on his face. A trip to the veterinarian revealed that he had red mange. Although it was treatable, he lost much of his hair and was quite pitiful. Angela could barely look at her little balding puppy. "Take him back. I don't want a sick puppy," she said.

Husband Mike replied, "Somebody's got to take care of the little fella." He was right.

The treatment for red mange required that Rocky be bathed daily and dipped in medication. The process took about six to eight weeks. During this recovery time, he lost most of his hair. When it finally began to grow back, his coat was luxuriously thick and beautiful.

Rocky had moved to a really good home. He was the baby and loved it! Allowed to sit on furniture and sleep in the bed, he enjoyed privileges that Gracie did not. Angela was a stay-at-home mom, plus Rocky had the attention of Matthew, as well as Mikey and Charli (the Britt's older son and his wife).

Rocky was much more laid back than Gracie. Not that he was perfect, mind you. Take, for example, the time he ate an entire pan of rising home-made bread dough when the family had gone to church. Or the day he devoured Mike's homemade beef jerky.

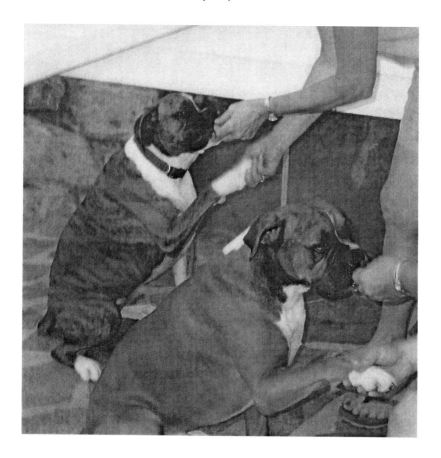

Hello Bro!

Rocky and Gracie had not seen each other in months. When we arrived at the Britt's home that Sunday evening, they were a little testy with one another. The connection was quickly made, though, and the games were on.

Angela, Mike, and I sat on their newly-constructed swing and watched the show. Gracie quickly established her dominance. Rocky was a gentleman and let her be the boss. He was a little bigger than Gracie, but he let her rule.

Their favorite games were chase, face wrestling, and tug-of-war. The tug-of-war often resulted in Gracie dragging Rocky down a slope in the backyard as he was lying down and hanging on to whatever they were tugging. Our job was to stay out of their way, as they often ran out of control. One time I had no idea Rocky was behind me when he literally took my legs out from under me and I landed on concrete. "Just keep them off of me," I said while trying to figure out if my body was still in one piece. It took my bruised elbow a couple of months to heal, but nothing was broken.

Occasionally we would have to stop their antics when someone was bleeding. It was usually a little puncture or scrape around the mouth area and playtime was resumed.

Rocky went nuts over a football. Mikey and Matthew would pass the football. Rocky ran back and forth, attempting an interception. Should one of the guys drop the ball, Rocky pounced. When the ball was in Rocky's possession, the brothers tried to get it back before Rocky punctured it. Gracie really didn't care about the football, but she loved chasing Rocky.

Many footballs were destroyed, as Rocky did not want to relinquish his catch.

Rocky developed his own game with a tennis ball. He would stand at the top of the driveway, drop the ball, and watch it roll down the driveway, into the street, and across the road. If Mike and Angela were outside, they would retrieve the tennis ball. In their absence, their neighbor, Mike, tossed the ball back. This became such a fun sport that Rocky even had people stop their cars, get out, and return the ball to him. He had us all trained!

Swallowing the Evidence

Once Rocky got his jaws on something, it was just about impossible to get it away from him. Mike had a technique that worked well. This consisted of putting pressure on the sides of his mouth until Rocky released the object. Rocky also found that if he could swallow whatever was in his mouth, he would not have to give it back. This just about cost him his life.

Mike is a very talented man who can fix just about anything. His garage is full of tools and just about anything else you would need. One day Rocky and Gracie found a rubber bulb in the garage. This proved to be a great toy. It was shaped like a light bulb and was about the size of an appliance bulb, but was soft. It was even more fun than the leather work gloves they played with. I suppose they had played with it for a couple of days.

One day Rocky was playing with it by himself. Angela noticed that he was putting it too far back in his mouth. She decided it was time to repossess it. Rocky decided it was time to swallow it. The bulb became lodged in his throat and he began to gasp for air. Angela panicked, screaming, "Take him to the vet!" There was no time for that. Fortunately, Mikey was there. His quick thinking and canine form of the Heimlich maneuver saved the day and Rocky's life. Disaster was averted and the bulb was thrown away.

While Rocky preferred footballs, Gracie loved to play with a baseball. It wasn't the fun of retrieving, it was the delight in removing the cover and attempting to eat it. The same went for leather gloves.

Gracie and Rocky were on flea preventative medication. After about a year, the formula quit working and, much to our surprise, they both had fleas. We treated the dogs successfully. The Britts also treated their yard. The chemicals not only killed fleas, but also brought hundreds of grub worms to the surface. Of course, Gracie simply could not resist them. Every day I would pick up grub worms and throw them away. She beat me to several of them and swallowed them.

My concern was the poison they contained, which had caused them to surface. I called a pet control poison center and was told that she had not ingested enough for it to be a problem.

Doggie delicacies: Leather gloves, baseball covers, rubber bulbs, metal scrubbies and grub worms!

Let It Bee!

It happened again today. Gracie snapped at a bumblebee and had it in her mouth. I screamed at her, she opened her mouth, and the bee attacked me. Armed with antihistamines, I waited for a reaction. Most of the time, she miraculously avoided being stung.

Bumblebees are really pretty amiable. They seem to endure abuse and go about their business. Wasps are another story. They do not appreciate any invasion of their air space. They are also masters at landing where you cannot reach them. All of a sudden your back hurts and swelling begins.

A yellow jacket wins the vengeance award. It's strange how you can safely mow your yard all spring and summer. Then, one day in August, you mow over a small hole that you did not even see, but soon find out that it is an entrance to the "nether regions."

Would that only one yellow jacket responded to your presence. Instead, it's all hands on deck as every available flyer joins the air force. Talk about pursuit! They are merciless to the point of chasing down the enemy and firing all available guns.

This is particularly dangerous to a dog. Their heads are closer to the ground and their feet have no extra skin to accommodate the swelling.

Now add to those facts the fact that Rocky and Gracie never seemed to learn. If it moved, they were going after it!

Sometimes you just have to let it bee!!!

Monkey See, Monkey Do

It happened again today. Angela met us at the car and proclaimed to Gracie, "You've been teaching my boy bad habits."

"What did he do now?" I replied sheepishly. Whatever he had done, I knew that Gracie would get the blame!

Angela went on to explain, "When I came home, Rocky met me at the door. I always know he's been up to something when he does that. It was like he had to tell me what had happened while I was gone and he had no idea how it happened. I went inside to find that he had emptied the trash can in the bathroom and had taken tissues into Matt's room. He never did that until he saw Gracie do it."

I really think that we were busted this time. For some unknown reason, Gracie just loved to snitch tissues from the bathroom trash can. In fact, we had to close the doors to the bathrooms when we visited Rocky. He had never attempted such mischief until he saw her do it.

Maybe he wanted to see how much fun it was. Perhaps there was some delicacy in the trash that day. Was it out of spite or revenge because Angela had left him alone? We'll never know. But this one thing we are sure of: Rocky IS taking his cues from Gracie. This is a dangerous thing. Why is it that bad behavior seems contagious, but they never pick up each other's good habits?

Happy Birthday!!!

Monday, August 22, 2011 was Gracie and Rocky's sixth birthday. We celebrated in grand style. First of all, we were able to be with her the entire day. That would be her number one request for a perfect day.

Gracie loved cookouts and steak was her favorite meal. The peach cobbler was more for us, but she loved tasting it.

The big celebration came at Rocky's. Being littermates, they shared the same birthday. On Gracie's gold bandana was written "Party Dawg, #6." Rocky's present was in a gift bag labeled "Happie burfday, bro." Inside was a very tough five-inch rubber ball with a rope sticking out of each end.

The Howell traditional canine birthday cake is made of prepared pancake mix enhanced with a jar of meat-flavored baby food. Beef flavor seemed just right for a couple of six-year-olds. The pancakes are made in the shape of the number that corresponds to the age of the birthday pup. My best friend, Carla, used to do this for her children, Brandon and Laura. Of course, she left the meat-flavored baby food out and served the numbered pancakes to her children for breakfast. This batch produced seven pancakes shaped like the number six. One was too large and fell apart as I attempted to flip it. We saved that one for later. This particular year, I added a special touch. The pancakes were fried in butter.

Six of the pancakes actually turned out to be recognizable as the number six. When they had fully cooled, I laid each one on a paper plate and stacked them on top of each other, placing waxed paper between layers.

Rocky had been anxious to open presents on Mike's birthday, which is on the 20th of August. After all, it IS all about Rocky, right? I figured that he would charge his gift bag immediately, but as we entered the room, Rocky got a whiff of the pancakes. I was certain that Angela never fed Rocky, as he literally attempted to dive into the pancakes. Two gulps and the number six pancake was history.

Gracie loved whipping cream from a can and I squirted some of that on her birthday pancake. At one point, she wore the whipped cream on her eyebrow. Rocky stood over her as she carefully ate the rest of her birthday pancake. They each enjoyed two puppy pancakes before turning their attention to the gifts.

Oh, the joy of tearing something open. However, tearing something open in front of another dog trumps that! Rocky's present was a great hit. Once he had gotten it out of the bag, he grabbed it and ran into the den, unwilling to share with Gracie. A game of king/queen of the couch began. We normally do not allow this game, but hey, it was their birthday! This was followed by fun and games outside and a meal of Gracie's favorite dog food.

Six years old! My, the time had passed quickly. Calculated in "Gracieville," she was now twelve-years-old. Rocky's age was calculated on a different scale. Today he had turned fifty-five. Sometimes I marvel that they are brother and sister!

The Woodchuck Family

How much wood could a woodchuck chuck if a woodchuck could chuck wood? Being around the Britt family, I had to revisit this question. Mike loves wood. He can make just about anything out of wood, including furniture. Attached to his garage is a woodworking shop with a room for drying and storing wood. Mike simply can't get enough of wood.

A wood stove keeps their home cozy and warm in the winter. Cutting, splitting, stacking, and storing the wood is a Britt tradition. When you cut your own wood, it warms you twice. The firewood is stacked against the chain-link fence in the back yard and reaches the top of the fence. Two rows deep, it measures anywhere from sixty to one hundred feet long. We call it the fortress.

We suspected that Rocky was part goat when he decided to climb to the top of the fortress and walk across it. He could have easily jumped out and landed on the other side of the fence, but walking the length of it and surveying his yard seemed to satisfy him. Gracie watched with wonder, but was not at all interested in joining him. Perhaps it is a Britt rite of passage . . .

Within the woodpile one could find an assortment of life, if one was determined to do so. Rocky and Gracie were determined. Mice and frogs were commonly found in the woodpile, and every now and then there was a snake in it. Gracie spent much time trying to dig into the woodpile, but was never able to capture any of the critters. For this I was thankful, as I love and respect all life. OK, I could do without the snakes!

The fortress of wood also provided a vast array of chewing material. Neither Rocky nor Gracie would eat the wood. They just chewed it up and made a mess.

Got Wood?
It's a Britt deal!
Actually, the Britts are more like a family of beavers!

Gracie's First Boyfriend

Gracie has always had a clear preference for men. When men and women were both present, she was drawn to the men. Perhaps this was because she soon learned that men tolerated her rambunctious nature better than women and actually seemed to enjoy the face-washings she dispensed. Maybe Angela marked her, as she would proclaim, "I don't like lickins. I don't like lickins." Gracie's attitude was, OK, so you don't like lickins. I'll just find somebody who does.

That someone was Matthew. Matthew is Angela's gown son who lived at home. He is an outstanding young man with high standards and a gentle nature, and Gracie was immediately drawn to him.

Many times I would be at the Britt's in the afternoon. Rocky and Gracie knew what time the Britt men were due home from work. The couch in the den was positioned under the window. From that vantage point, they could see who pulled into the driveway. Matthew was the first one home. Oh, the excitement and delight of "You're home!" They danced with delight to see Matthew. There is simply nothing like a doggie "welcome home."

Now Gracie had a huge tongue and she knew how to work it. It seemed to run the length of her body and attach to her bobble so that everything wagged in unison. Matthew gladly received her hugs and kisses. She simply adored him. It wasn't long before Matthew called Gracie "my girl." There was plenty of Gracie to go around and we were more than glad to share her.

Matthew and I became great friends. I claimed to be his big sister. Actually, I was less like an older sister and more like a little sister, as he towered over me. I'm not sure how this was possible, as his mom, Angela, was younger than I was. We spent many Saturdays riding bikes on the Virginia Creeper Trail.

Matt and Gracie had a special bond. Once Norma, who is now his wife, came into the picture, Gracie didn't see as much of her beloved Matthew. But then she gained a new friend as she welcomed Norma into the pack.

Advice from a Dog

When loved ones come home, always run to greet them
Be loyal
Delight in the simple joys of a long walk
Unleash your talents
Hide your favorite snack
Make new friends
Learn new tricks no matter what your age

The Lap Dogs

Rocky was a cuddle bug. At the tender age of six weeks, he loved being wrapped up in a blanket and resting on Angela's lap. During his illness, he was cuddled even more and he enjoyed every moment of it. As he grew and grew, he continued to be a lap dog. There is a huge difference in a six-pound lap dog and an eighty-pound lap dog . . . but not to Rocky. Angela spent many hours rocking her baby boy. I often wondered if that was why they had named him Rocky.

He loved the recliner and the couch. Unlike Rocky, Gracie could rarely be still enough to sit on a lap. She had developed a fear of thunderstorms and very loud noises, and sought the safety of a lap at such times. During a thunderstorm I would have both of them on my lap. It was, indeed, a tight squeeze and I was the one being squeezed. Occasionally Rocky would shift his weight and move toward the back of the recliner. This resulted in "man overboard," as the chair tipped backward and hit the floor. Rocky was thrilled, as his person was now lying down and he had access to that person's face. A second person was required to rescue the victim of the accident.

Rocky and Gracie were lap dogs in another way, too. They absolutely loved to chase one another. In fact, I think it was their favorite game. I'm not sure how they determined who was the chaser and who became the chased, but, somehow, in doggie language that was communicated. Gracie usually started it with Rocky in pursuit. Many times they made laps around the house. Each lap Rocky would drop further behind until he would finally double back to reach her. Our job was to stay out of the way because, at this point, they were running out of control.

One morning I noticed that Gracie could barely get in the car to go for our walk. When she got out, she didn't want to move. She seemed to be in pain. I took her to the vet and found she had sprained her shoulder. When I mentioned this to Angela she replied, "Didn't you see it?"

"See what?" I asked.

"The collision."

I asked, "What collision?" She told me that Rocky and Gracie had been running full tilt the previous evening when they'd had a full-force, head-on collision. Rocky was about fifteen pounds heavier than Gracie, so she had taken the brunt of the blow. Gracie tolerated pain very well. She never cried out or whimpered. I'd had no idea that they had collided. She had continued to play. Play was always at the top of her list. The soreness caught up to her the next day. A few days of rest healed the soreness and she was back on track.

Rocky appreciated "the growly bites." He understood that it was all in good fun. Gracie was definitely the dominant of the two and he was fine with that fact. Rocky lived about seven minutes away from us and Gracie soon learned the road to Rocky's house. She would begin to squeal with delight when we were about halfway there. When we arrived, the games began. Face wrestling, tug-of-war, and chase served to get the monkeys out of Rocky and remove the grazillas from Gracie. When we came home, she was tired. A tired boxer is a good boxer.

Rocky was the original "Commando Raider." When he was little, he would flatten himself out as much as possible and wiggle underneath the bed. This provided a place to hide and a very secure cave. He quickly outgrew his secret headquarters, but his mission as a commando raider continued. He taught Gracie the position. During their frequent games of chase, each would have to assume the commando raider posture when they ran underneath the boat. Matthew and Mikey's boats spent the winter on a carport at Angela's home. We cringed whenever they shimmied under the boat, hoping that they would not conk their heads. Of course, their heads were so hard that they may have damaged the boat!

It's hard to make a bunny rabbit out of a wolverine!

Sunday Dinner

After Sunday morning church, Angela prepared a big dinner for her family. Gracie and I would visit after the meal and eventually joined them for Sunday dinner. This became a three-ring begging circus.

Mikey and Charli now had their own dog, a Rottweiler named Von Bearenstein Bear, but known as "Bear." And a bear he is! Bear lived to eat. The runt of the litter, apparently he'd had trouble getting his share of food and was still working to make up for that fact.

Gracie was always a delicate eater. Rocky was mannerly unless he could snitch something off the table. Bear was the enthusiastic, vivacious one of the three. You had to be very careful how you fed tidbits to Bear, lest he bite your fingers as he took the food. He would often intercept food intended for Rocky or Gracie. Mikey had taught Bear to be "easy," but he had to be constantly reminded.

While the family was assembled at the table, the canines took their places. It didn't take three dogs long to figure out who the soft touches were at the dinner table. Mike was the most generous with his offerings. Gracie positioned herself on one side of Mike while Bear, who may have had a vacuum inside his stomach, stood at the other side, placing his drooling mouth on Mike's leg. Gracie was mannerly as she sat and begged. Should Mike take too long between offerings, she would raise her paw to shake hands. She had learned that humans could be taught to be Pez dispensers if she looked cute enough. All three dogs knew to sit and shake hands and that they would be rewarded for doing so. Bear would often force his long muzzle between someone's arm and ribs. This was his way of reminding us that he was still there and was not full yet. Bear never seemed to get full and he would eat anything that did not eat him first.

In fact, Bear ate many things he should not have. When I pooper-scooped the yard, I always knew which ones were Bear's because they were in Technicolor. Strings, foil, corn, rope, stuffing from toys, paper . . . somehow it all just passed through him. He did eventually wind up having to have emergency surgery, as he finally ate something that swelled inside his digestive system.

Rocky was the polite eater. But then he knew he could have anything he wanted the other six days of the week!

SOS

And then there was the Sunday dinner when Mike grilled steaks outside. Angela had prepared wonderful side dishes and everyone's tummies were full. Mikey, being the good son that he is, was gracious enough to go outside and clean the grill. Following closely behind him were Gracie and Bear. I stayed inside to help clean up the dishes.

Several minutes later Mikey came in and announced, "Gracie ate the SOS pad." What! No! Surely she hadn't! Not my "dogter." I can see it all now. The pad had the smell of steak on it. Mikey had put it down. Gracie had looked at Bear and Bear had looked at Gracie, and then the chase had begun! Apparently she had won. Of course, she'd had to swallow it to keep him from getting the treasure.

I can only imagine what it must feel like to have a metal dish washing scrubby go down your throat! How in the world? Why in the world? What had she been thinking? How had it slid down? I expected it would come right back up. I prayed it would come right back up. She did spit up a little bit, but no SOS pad.

I laid hands on her and prayed. Oh Lord, please protect her digestive system. Oh Lord, please, I don't want to have to tell Larry about this. Of course it was Sunday and the vet's office was closed. She acted like she felt fine and I halfway forgot about it.

At about 3:30 the next morning she came to my side of the bed to let me know that she needed to go outside. I put on a robe and went into the hall and stepped on something cold, wet and squishy. Thank you, Lord. It was the SOS pad. Now imagine how it must have felt coming back up her esophagus! I quickly recovered the contraband and threw it in the trash.

How thankful I am that He answered my prayers. She was fine and, unless he reads this book, Larry will never know!

Swimming Pool Personalities

You can tell a lot about a dog just by watching it play in a child's plastic swimming pool. Rocky, Gracie, and Bear each had their own pool and gladly shared. The following is an assessment of their pool personalities.

The Agitator: This dog acts like an agitator in a washing machine. He digs at the bottom of the pool, splashing wildly. He rolls over in the water, even submerging his head. His entire body gets soaked. He appears to be trying to walk on water, but this never works. The agitator doesn't give up. He simply must get to the bottom of things. By the time he comes out of the pool, you may need to add more water. Bear is an agitator.

Tippecanoe (or the pansy): Tippecanoe is not afraid of the pool, but he only wants to drink from it. If it is very hot outside or he is very tired, he will very carefully place his front feet in the water to cool his toes. This dog is definitely the most laid back. He is Mr. Ho Hum of the pool personalities. Rocky is Tippecanoe or the pansy.

The Little Dipper: The little dipper is somewhere between the agitator and Tippecanoe. She delights in the pool and frequently uses it during hot weather. Entering with all four feet in the water, she carefully dips her chest down for cooling refreshment. Having accomplished the cooling-off process, she gladly shares by shaking herself. Now everyone is refreshed! Elizabeth Grace is the little dipper.

What's your swimming pool personality? Each one is a unique expression of who we are!

Loaded for Bear

Gracie simply must have her exercise. In the morning a walk will suffice. By midafternoon, she starts to lose it. The need for hard, rough, and tumble, chase and run, hide and seek, and good old-fashioned face wrestling becomes apparent. We call this reaching "critical mass."

Today was Sunday. I had been gone for the majority of the previous day, which broke rule number one. Before I left for church, I took her outside. The growly bities came on her with a vengeance. Or should I say the growly bities came on me! Fur with an attitude went into action. My previous technique did not work. She was really peeved with me. I managed to escape by going to church, but I knew that when I returned she HAD to have some serious exercise.

At lunchtime that day the phone rang. Mikey told me that he, Charli, and Bear were at Rocky's and wondered if we were coming up. I don't know who needed whom more, but Bear and Gracie needed some action. It was obviously a "bear of a day."

When we arrived at the Britt's, I announced that Gracie was "loaded for Bear." Bear and Gracie had not seen each other in a week. Gracie had to first remind Bear of her dominance. She accomplished this by jumping on Bear, growling, and pinning him down just because he'd had his tongue on the cake on the counter. After a stern rebuke from me, they both were sent outside to play.

All was forgiven and the fun began. Bear was younger and larger than Gracie, but she gave him a run for his money. Rocky did his best to stay out of their way. While Gracie was loaded for Bear, Rocky was loaded for gold-fish. This was his default mode.

Sometimes you have to be loaded for bear!

Just Wondering

Although Gracie was spayed, I often wondered what Bear and Gracie's puppies would be like. They would certainly be rambunctious, rowdy, stubborn, and mischievous. They may have had an opera voice like Bear or rarely bark at all, like Gracie. They probably would not have been ideal pets. But what would we have called them? Rottenboxers or Boxweilers?

Gracie rarely barked. In fact, I was frequently asked if she could bark. Somehow, in her happy secure world she simply did not feel the need to be vocal. Bear was just the opposite. He went beyond barking. His operatic serenades were loud and high pitched. I'm so grateful that he did not teach her how to sing!

You know your boxer is tired when you open the refrigerator door and she doesn't come running or when you can mop the floor without interference.

It's All in the Family

Rocky and Gracie were born brother and sister. And, somehow through the goodness of God, the Britts also became family to us. Our daily visits were enjoyable as we watched our youngsters grow and play together. During this time a bond of love was developing between the two families.

Mike is Mr. Fix it. I only remember one item that I destroyed beyond his ability to repair. A family of hard workers, the Britts helped Larry and me with many projects, including cutting down trees, leveling our outdoor building, building a stone wall, and hauling landscaping rocks to our home. Matthew and Mikey were young and strong and helped us with some heavy-duty projects.

We had many interesting discussions. I learned a lot about Freewill Baptists. I know I really stretched Mike, especially during our conversations concerning certain Scriptures—namely those about women. We must have had a particularly lively discussion one day. The following day, I exited my car in silence, carrying this sign:

Hi!
My name is "Nospeakalot"
Can I sit on your porch awhile with my dog?
Enjoy!
Let the women learn in silence!

Of course, this did not last long!

PVC for You and Me!

Plastic PVC pipe is kind of like duct tape. It's absolutely amazing what you can use it for. Rocky, Bear, and Grace learned that PVC can be sheer delight.

I think it was Mike who first had the idea, or perhaps they just happened to find a piece of PVC pipe in the yard one day. However it happened, I have never seen three dogs so delighted by such a simple toy.

First of all, it was slippery and a little difficult for them to get their mouths on. Once they mastered the art of holding it, the games were on. It was not suitable for tug-of-war but it worked fine when the three of them carried it around the yard together. Gracie usually dropped it first, as her mouth was smaller than the boys' mouths.

Often they would carry it side by side, leaving one end loose. The pipe was about eight feet long and perhaps an inch in diameter. The free end produced a whiplike effect, which found unsuspecting legs at about the calf muscle or knee. Depending on how fast the dogs were moving, this resulted in anything from a bump to a full-fledged ouch!

The pipe amused them for hours. Should they lay it down, Mike would pick up an end and make a sound through it. This caused excitement as they looked for the cause of the mysterious sound.

Rocky was, indeed, a most lovable dog. He was not, however, the sharpest knife in the drawer. His intelligence bump simply did not exist. When Rocky decided to bring the PVC pipe in the house, he just could not figure out how to get it past the porch posts. When he attempted to carry it horizontally, the pipe hit the porch post every time. He never made it to the door. This proved to be a blessing for Angela's collection of knick-knacks.

Oh, for the simple things in life. What joy they can bring us!

The Jigsaw Puzzles

During the winter, we all stayed inside more. One winter in particular, we began putting together jigsaw puzzles at the Britt's house. We placed a large piece of lightweight wood over the table, which gave us room to spread the pieces out and would accommodate the finished product. Mike and I enjoyed the challenge of putting something together. Angela was the audience/supervisor and occasionally suggested a piece. Whoever came to visit was welcome to work on it.

Rocky and Gracie amused themselves as we worked piece by piece. They were never far from us and it was not unusual for the board to suddenly be lifted up as the dogs came up under it. Should one of us drop a piece on the floor, the mad scramble began. This added a new dimension to our activity, as quickness was a valuable asset. It became a game of who would pick it up first. Being lower to the ground, Rocky and Gracie were often the winners.

Retrieving the piece from Gracie's mouth was easy. She might leave a slight tooth mark on the piece, but it was always usable. Rocky did not surrender his prey easily. His powerful jaws made deep tooth marks. The longer it stayed in his possession, the wetter the puzzle piece became. The wetter it became, the more the piece swelled.

One puzzle was never completed. There were two pieces that were not found. I'm quite sure they wound up in Rocky's tummy.

Love Those Guys!

Gracie's preference for men was evident to everyone. She would leave Jan, her friend at the cell phone store, and take up with a male customer who was a stranger to her. In time, we figured out why.

There are a number of men who love to have a dog lick their faces. Gracie was more than glad to accommodate them. After Gracie had dispensed a complete facial bath to someone she had just met, the man told me "Those are the best kisses I've had in a long time." A man with facial hair was especially interesting to Gracie.

Gracie had a tongue that simply would not quit. Matthew and Mike graciously accepted her huge tongue and Gracie's excitement grew with each lick. Once or twice Matthew wound up on the ground and received the complimentary body bath. Mike and Matthew had their techniques for surviving the ordeal. They would squinch their eyes shut and cover their mouths. Everything else was fair game.

Repairmen who came to our home were greeted by Gracie. Most of them delighted in her affection. Our plumbers were always glad to see her and accept her freely given affection. She was truly an affection dispenser.

Most women will not tolerate this. My friend Debbie is the exception. She, like the guys, loved the show of affection. Good old boxer jumps and leaps often accompanied the greeting. During one of Debbie's visits, I heard the sound of her upper teeth hitting her lower teeth. Gracie had jumped up, hitting her head on Debbie's jaw. I wondered how much dentures would cost. Somehow, Debbie survived the blow.

"You choose the licking-est dogs." — Matthew Britt

The Snitchit

Although Gracie was tall enough to reach the kitchen counter, she never attempted to remove anything from it. One day I had made cornbread muffins in little paper muffin cups. I left them to cool on the counter.

Sometime later, I returned to the kitchen and counted the muffins. Two of them were missing. I asked Larry if he had eaten them. No, he had not. My investigation began. I found a few muffin crumbs on the dining room floor and on Gracie's face. She had eaten them, paper and all. This earned her the title "The Muffin Meister." From this point on, anything on the counter was of interest to her. Food had to be placed way back on the counter, which was out of her reach

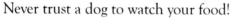

Never trust a dog to watch your food!

Pain In the Neck

Gracie was suffering from the double monkeys. Just before her condition escalated to the grazillas, we headed for Bear's house. Sometimes Rocky is sufficient action, but today was a bear of a day.

Arriving at Bear's in the afternoon, we observed that the double monkeys had found another victim. We needed to go outside as soon as possible! These pups needed space!

Gracie and Bear were in fine form as they ran and chased on the ragged edge of control. I was very careful to stay out of their way, at least until the initial excitement subsided. Finding a shaded area in the yard, I moved a lightweight plastic chair about four feet from the solid wooden fence. Gracie and Bear were having a blast. Thinking that everything was under control, I immersed myself in paperwork. Suddenly I felt my chair rise slightly. Before another thought could cross my mind (like "get up"), the two front legs of the chair were lifted off the ground. As the chair tilted back, I reached back with my left hand. This broke the force of the blow to my neck and also knocked a chunk of skin out of my hand. My neck slammed into the fence, producing trauma to two vertebrae and great pain. Crashing to the right side, I was met by two slurpy tongues more than glad to assist me.

"Get off! Just get away!" I commanded. The pain was severe enough to make me sick and a little woozy. Bear and Gracie backed off enough to give me breathing room. Once I determined that I was still alive and all body parts were working, I climbed to my feet. Laying my hands on my neck, I prayed for complete and total healing.

Stumbling inside the house, I quickly iced my neck and began the futile search for a band-aid. Blood was dripping from my right forearm. The ice pack worked well and the neck pain eased. It was only then that I realized how much my left hand hurt.

The hooligans were outside, having a grand time. My head was still pretty fuzzy, so I called for a back up unit. Thankful that Larry was home, I asked him to bring band-aids and our automatic car. He and Gracie could travel in my five speed and follow me home as a precautionary measure.

While I was awaiting his arrival, my best friend, Carla, called me to explain the predicament she was in. Remodeling her laundry room and bathroom was turning into a major overhaul. The next day we were scheduled to begin a four-day praise camp for children. Carla found herself with no running water and her house was upside down.

"What are you doing?" she asked.

"I just had an accident," I replied. I proceeded to tell her about my neck and the other injuries. "And why should we be surprised?" I asked. Praise camp started tomorrow. We knew old slew foot wasn't going to take that lying down. Realizing who were up against filled us with resolve to fight the good fight of faith and move forward. We called in prayer support and pressed on!

I called my chiropractor, Scott. He wanted to see me right away. I explained to him what had happened and that it was the day before praise camp was to begin. "Where I go to church, we call that spiritual warfare," he said. Yep! You got it!

I learned some valuable lessons from this fiasco.

1. Never sit in a lightweight chair when one or more boisterous dogs are around.
2. Be on guard when you are about to invade the enemy's territory.
3. Resist the enemy and he will flee from you.

Footnote: Praise camp went on as scheduled. About forty children attended and experienced worship and learned to express their hearts through dance, banners, processionals, raising flags, and waving streamers. A ten-year-old named Madison was born again. I was able to share this testimony when I learned that one of the children had fallen while dancing and had injured her knee.

When you fall down, get up and move on!
Satan can just shut up and sit down!
Gracie and Bear, whose side are you on anyway???

Pastor Marvin said in one of his sermons:
"I need more grace at my house"
To which I replied,
"When can I bring her and how long can she stay?"

Why Do We Love Her?

And then there was the day when Gracie had been extremely difficult. She had worn Larry's nerves to a frazzle. He asked the question "Why do we love her?" She had been stubborn and relentlessly demanding. We were both tired and our nerves had been stretched to the limit from the workday.

I thought carefully about his question. Just why do we love her? First of all, we had chosen her and made her our own. We had paid the price for her (and still do everyday). We had invested in her. We had removed her from the doggie kingdom and had placed her in the human realm to dwell with us. We were committed to her care and connected to her. True, she could be totally charming, and she was a beauty, but our love went far beyond that.

If beauty is as beauty does, you can discount the good looks factor. As I pondered our love for her, I saw it was all based on us, not her behavior or looks. The very meaning of her name, "Grace," was unmerited favor. We loved her based on what we were, not on what she was.

So it is with God's love for us. It's all based on who He is. He chose us and made us His own. He paid the price and has so much invested in us. He's committed to our care.

True love is a gift—grace given by one who has the ability to abundantly give. We can never be good enough to earn His grace. Thank you, Lord, for your great love to us!

Dogs have it all together.
They know who their master is.
They expect their master to come.
They wait and lean upon their master.

The Helpmeet and the Helpmeat

Men are so blessed. God created someone very special for Adam. Eve was formed from Adam's rib so he would not be alone. Her purpose was to be a helpmeet and companion for him.

God also created the dog. Many say that the dog is man's best friend. DOG is actually GOD spelled backwards. While I am Larry's helpmeet, Gracie is his helpmeat. Chicken is her very favorite. Whenever it is thawing, cooking, or cooling, she whines intermittently for "just a morsel from the master's table." Beef or turkey will do just fine, thank you.

It didn't take Gracie long to figure out that Larry was also her snacking buddy. Anytime he headed for the kitchen to snack, she was right there with him. The sound of a squirt can of whipping cream is more effective than calling her name.

She joins us at the table and sits on the floor, stationed between us. As we give thanks, she patiently waits for her share of the meal. She will eat any meat, pasta, or dessert. We can keep the fruits and vegetables.

Cookouts are her favorite, as she gets her own beef hot dog, small hamburger, or a serving of steak. She also likes marshmallows. Anything dropped on the floor is fair game. Oh, by the way, her popcorn must be slathered in butter. She quickly learned to beg popcorn from me because Larry eats his unbuttered.

Be who God created you to be

And

Fulfill your destiny!

Boxer Soup

Warning: Plays with Food!

Gracie is the only canine chef we have ever had. Her specialty is boxer soup. Here's the recipe:

1. Eat your entire bowl of food. Make sure that plenty of it sticks on your face.
2. Proceed immediately to the water bowl.
3. Immerse your muzzle in enough water to loosen and remove all crumbs from your face.

If properly mixed, you now have boxer soup. Food particles should be floating and submerged in the water bowl.

Now the fun begins. Catch and eat the food crumbs out of the water. This is somewhat like bobbing for apples. Hint: Sunken food will rise to the top when bubbles are blown in the water (Yes, she actually does this).

When a large puddle forms on the floor, humans will intervene and stop the game to dump out the water. This means that the boxer has won!

It's all about Grace!

Boxer Bowling

Larry was a bowling enthusiast in years gone by. His perfect 300 game and 809 set of three games are accomplishments we are proud of. In human bowling, a score of 300 is a perfect game. A 300 game is thirteen strikes in a row. The higher the score, the better the game. Boxer bowling is different.

I believe the motivation of boxer bowling is boredom with a need for attention. And, a little hunger is a great motivator as well. The fewer "pins" you knock down, the more successful the game is.

Gracie's food and water dishes are in an elevated rack. Behind this rack, we store two-liter drinks. These are the pins. For Gracie to access the pins, she must go underneath the kitchen table, turn, and head towards the hutch.

Sometimes the offerings in her water or food bowl simply do not meet her standards. The water must be freshly drawn from our reverse osmosis filtration system. Any attempt to serve subpar meals will be met with her disapproval. It's not unusual for her to paw, whine, or cry at the bowls. Not one to be overlooked, when these tactics are ignored, she may resort to boxer bowling.

Boxer bowling is not as much fun as it is self-serving. Entering one of her caves underneath the kitchen table, she sneaks up on her prey. Unlike human bowling, the pins do not need to be arranged in a particular pattern. Using her nose, she knocks one of the two-liter bottles over. If immediate action is not taken, she will continue knocking the "pins" down. Gracie always wins. Either she gets what she wants or all of the pins are rolling across the floor and she gets attention.

How often do we humans play boxer bowling? Can't have my way? Clunk . . . over goes a pin. Ignore me? Crash. Let me send another one rolling.

It's a stark contrast to what Paul said. In Philippians 4:12, he said, "For I have learned, in whatsoever state I am, therewith to be content."

The Smooch Patrol

There seems to be a rule in the doggie kingdom that reads: No one in the house gets affection except the dog. It also seems that it is the assigned task of the resident dog to enforce this rule.

Any kissing, hugging, or other forms of affection will result in an intervention or interception of said affection by the "Smooch Patrol." Being the only dog in our household, Gracie is our resident enforcer. She takes this assignment seriously. Her methods of enforcement vary according to the severity of the infraction.

The Look: This method is rarely used simply because it is not effective.

The Paw: The paw is a powerful weapon for a boxer. With it, they speak volumes. "The paw," when administered by the smooch patrol, means "break it up."

The Face: This is the cutest, most gentle form of enforcement offered by the smooch patrol officer. Gracie demonstrated this technique just last week. She was asleep under the dining room table. Larry and I were playing a board game. A few innocent pecks on the lips resulted in a smooch patrol alarm. We looked down to see her skunk-striped face nestled between us. It's a great technique. The people laugh and quit the mushy stuff.

Full-Body Intervention: Occasionally an extreme technique is required. Bodies simply must be separated. The canine's long, smooth structure is the perfect tool. Gracie is experienced at this and has it down to an art. It may begin with "the look," followed by a low growl or "the paw," and is completed by squeezing her body between ours.

Of course, we all know, it's all about Gracie! Our home is truly full of Grace!

Good Morning, Gracie!

The first human body to vacate the bed will be replaced by Gracie. We are careful to replace the covers and put her softie on the spot she is soon to occupy.

Larry was the first person out of bed on this particular morning. After he had gotten up, Gracie moved from "Gracie's place" on the foot of the bed to her new position. She was quite close to the edge. By this time, I was sitting up in bed and Larry, who had just delivered my morning coffee and a toaster waffle, was standing at the foot of the bed.

Gracie quickly fell asleep again. I often wonder what she dreams about. As she sleeps, she will twitch her eyes and mouth. Actually, she twitches her whole face. Sometimes she whines or kicks. This morning she started to jerk. All four legs were flaying when, before we could reach out to her, she rolled off the bed, then crashed into the wall and the baseboard heater.

Good morning, Gracie! What a way to wake up! Hurt and confused, she wondered, "What happened?" Most of us don't enjoy rolling out of bed, but this was no way to start a day. Gracie is rarely timid or sheepish, but being awakened by an accident caused her to lower her ears and exhibit a defeated spirit. She slinked over to Larry for emotional support. Once assured that the roof had not caved in, she placed her chin on the bed and just looked at me.

"Come on up," I encouraged.

"Fool me once, shame on you, fool me twice, shame on me," she seemed to communicate. There was no way she was going to get back on that dangerous bed! Somehow I convinced her to return to the bed. Having learned a lesson, she positioned herself way over on my side.

Desiring to calm her fears, I gladly relinquished my position. Love does that, you know. Love gives. Love bends. Love never fails. Love seeks to please and brings comfort and peace. In the aftermath of crisis, love prevails.

Away In a Manger

The children at church had enjoyed holding baby Jesus during our Christmas presentation. I had borrowed a baby doll and manger from my best friend, Carla, who happens to be a children's minister. Ah, the gift of borrowing and the joy of having a best friend who could get her hands on just about anything I needed to use!

The time had come to return little baby Jesus to His rightful owner. Since Carla and I both were working and were unable to exchange Him in person, I was going to leave Him outside my house so that she could pick Him up.

The plan was quite simple. I was to leave baby Jesus on our carport. Carla was to come and pick Him up and return Him to His rightful place. Just in case Larry was the first one home from work, he was forewarned that baby Jesus was on the carport.

It was a great plan, except that Carla did not come on Monday . . . or Tuesday. On Tuesday afternoon I answered the phone at work and heard my exasperated husband announce, "Gracie's got baby Jesus in the backyard and she's getting Him dirty. I don't know if she's chewed on Him or not. It's not my fault!" Fault? Who said anything about fault? Why was it necessary to place blame on anybody? Let's just deal with the facts and future. The rest was history.

I assured Larry that it would be OK. The worst that could happen was that I would have to buy a new doll. OK, so forget the fact that the doll had been Carla's twenty-three-year-old daughter's childhood doll.

Gracie was thrilled that baby Jesus had come to her carport. He was an unexpected visitor and she took Him to herself. Delighted that no people were around to repossess her treasure, she carried Him with her and thoroughly enjoyed His company . . . until Larry decided to check on her. He was horrified to find her in the backyard with baby Jesus.

If you seek Him, you will find Him

How often are we guilty of her misdemeanor? We desire His company, yet we do not respect His presence. We say we want to walk with Him, yet we continue to go to places we know He would not choose to go.

Never Give Up

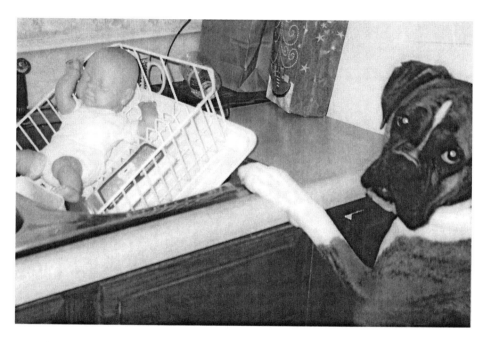

The damage done to baby Jesus was minimal. A careful examination proved that a good bath would make things right again.

Bath time has never been Gracie's favorite event. This time was different, though. She had had such a good time with baby Jesus. Somehow He wound up on the top of the refrigerator, one of the few places in our home totally out of her reach. Now the smell of the vinyl, the remembrance of a good time, and the lust of the "fur" renewed her excitement.

I carefully placed the doll in my kitchen sink and washed all of its vinyl parts. This removed every trace of the ordeal. Gracie watched with fascination and delight. I suppose that in her mind, I was preparing baby Jesus for another round of fun.

Once He was clean again, I patted the doll dry. The dish drainer seemed like an appropriate place to complete the drying process, but it was not quite out of Gracie's reach.

Gracie's crying and whining did not convince me to return the doll to her. Suddenly her front paws landed on the kitchen counter, giving her a closer look. He was so close . . . if she could just get me to understand what she wanted!

Often, what we want is simply not right for us. Cry and whine as we might, it's just not in our best interest. It's time to give it up, trust our Father, and move on.

The Test

It was November 28, one day before I had determined to turn in my notice of retirement. The mission of the day: put up the Christmas tree and decorations.

The participants were myself and Elizabeth Grace, who was now two years old. The game began as I carried boxes of decorations down from the attic. You must understand that with a boxer, everything is a game. So let's try football. I survived seven or eight trips down the stairs as Gracie foot tackled me.

Hide and seek was the next game. Gracie removed numerous ornaments from the boxes and carried them to various places in the house. The basket of pound puppies on the hearth was of special interest to her. She chose the brown one and placed it on her bed, then took a short, but much appreciated, nap.

Gracie was fascinated with a green velvet Christmas stocking that had a bear hanging out of it. She climbed on the couch in pursuit and was greeted with several firm "nos". She autographed her own stocking with tooth marks and repeatedly removed a small stuffed lamb ornament to claim as her own. A wild boxer bolt between the dining room table and Christmas tree took down four ornaments.

Did I really want to quit work and stay home with her? What a test! Often the best way to deal with Gracie is to change the pace. It was time to eat lunch and work on outside decorations. The great outdoors provided a much-needed reprieve. I was able to put up the outdoor lights and Gracie had a blast outside.

Yes, I really AM ready to quit my job. December 31 will be my last day. Yippee yi aye!

I am very much looking forward to the rest of my life. I actually AM ready to spend more time with Gracie and enjoy her company!

Highly esteem those whom God has entrusted to your care.

With Me Always

Dogs never cease to amaze me. Even the most rambunctious possess sensitivity when their master is needy.

I am rarely sick. Even when I am, I can almost always rise to the occasion and keep Gracie's exercise routine intact. Not this time. I spent most of three days in bed or on the couch.

I have never seen Gracie any sweeter. She gladly gave up her morning walks to be at my side. Whatever room I occupied, she stayed right with me. If I was able to be outside in the sunshine, she laid with her head on my feet. Larry and I were both amazed at her calmness and excellent behavior.

It helped that I was just barely able to take her to Bear's house each afternoon. He did an outstanding job "de-monkey-fying" her. When we returned home, she was ready for more rest time. I was very impressed until the double monkeys began to surface.

It started at Bear's house the third afternoon of my illness. Frustrated, she body blocked me, nearly knocking me over. By now, I actually had an audible voice with which to scold her. She backed up and decided to take it out on Bear. She simply could not hold it in any longer and I was so thankful that Bear was available to absorb her boxer energy.

The relationship between a dog and her master beautifully reflects that of ours with the Master. One of the meanings of worship is to give affection, as a dog licks his master's hand. Their joy is just to be with their master. The master's agenda becomes the dog's agenda.

Just to be in the Master's presence is a delight!

Grace Week

Those of us who live near Bristol, Tennessee know the meaning of Race Week. Racecar drivers roll into town and Thunder Valley rumbles with the sound of oval track racing engines. Aggressive drivers attempt to conquer the .558-mile track. The 2011 race week was also "Grace Week."

Turning six years old requires at least a week of celebration. The pre-grace event for Saturday was Gracie's introduction to a beautiful German shepherd. Rin Tin Tin was one of my childhood loves and this dog could have passed for "Rinny." His stature reminded me of the stuffed canine hero I had owned and cherished as child. He had been in a laying down position and had had a plastic molded face. He had been the closest thing I'd had to a dog until Taffy, the cocker spaniel, came to live with us.

I was shopping at a local store that allowed pets. Gracie delighted in all the attention she received on such an outing. She was usually very well behaved unless she saw another dog.

I saw him first and tightened my grip on the leash. The owner informed me that her dog was a gentle male and got along well with other dogs. Under close supervision, Gracie and the shepherd did the normal "getting to know you" techniques of sniffing and smelling that only dogs understand. Gracie was usually quite bossy, but she had enough doggie smarts to behave nicely when outsized. She soon became comfortable with her new friend and started boxing. German Shepherds apparently don't understand or appreciate this method of play. Her new friend decided that he had had enough of her antics.

We separated the pups and continued shopping. All were content except Gracie. She kept pulling towards her friend, asking for another chance. He certainly wasn't overjoyed with her persistence, but agreed to submit to another round. Without provocation, she snapped at him. He responded with a growl. We decided that was enough.

You're never gonna find a boyfriend like that, Gracie. It seems that the racecar drivers aren't the only ones with aggression issues!

Sunday of Grace Week

We were late for our Sunday morning walk and missed meeting our friend, Lowell. It was a typical walk and we had no problems. I went to church as usual and returned home for lunch. I had a meeting at church scheduled for 2:30 p.m. Somehow, in Gracieville, I am allowed only one trip away in the a.m. and another after 6:00 p.m. The 2:30 p.m. meeting simply did not fit into her plans.

That evening I drained and cleaned the hot tub. Someone was not getting enough attention. Did I say "act out"?

Gracie often vented her frustration in ugly ways. Attacking from the rear, Gracie went into the growly bitie mode. I managed to avoid the body slam, but she did grab my waist. No physical harm was done, but she managed to step on my last nerve. Where was the water hose when you needed it? Squirting her with water always worked to break the growly bities. When she felt the water on her back, she went into the trapezoidian run. I fended her off long enough to get back to the porch. A little attention calmed her down. Are we practicing for the race, or what?

I can't say that I remember anything special about Monday.

Tuesday

Tuesday was a calm and peaceful day. At 7:00 p.m. we headed out the back door to go to Rocky's house for some playtime. I was careful to look out the door before I let Gracie out. Although she was contained to the yard by an invisible fencing system (also known as "the buzzards"), I could not be too careful since I lived on the edge of the woods.

I opened the back door and Gracie bolted out. As she ran toward the woods, I expected to see the deer or a cat. Instead I heard a loud noise that sounded like barking coming from the edge of the woods. Gracie came to a screeching halt. She stopped well short of the underground fencing system boundaries. Something had really gotten her attention. Someone had instantly earned her respect.

I called her to the car and closed her inside. Investigating the incident, I walked toward the woods. I could see a doe about thirty feet away, just waiting. Gracie had never been intimidated by the deer. Perhaps she sneaked up on one of the fawns and mom let her have it . . . perhaps. . . .

Wednesday

Our morning walk was quite interesting. We stopped at our local banks, where the girls provided Gracie with treats. We headed for another one of her favorite places, the Express Care, and stopped to talk with owner, Greg, about renting his log cabin at the lake.

Bobby was working today. I asked him if deer could make a barking noise. He and Robby informed me that deer could grunt or snort, but not bark. Bobby then mentioned that a bear could bark just like a dog. Oh, a bear!

Although I had never seen a bear on our property, at least two other people had. Yes, I think a bear would have stopped Elizabeth Grace in her tracks! It was August, the time of year bears started "fattening up" for the winter. We did feed the birds, squirrels, raccoons, deer, and whatever else might help itself to our offerings of corn and birdseed.

Larry investigated and found many scratch marks on the concrete slab near the woods. The most telling one had four scratches together. They had been made by toenails, large toenails. Um, let's say claws, large claws. We were still in the fact-finding phase but I think we had a bear!

Captain Hook

Thursday's walk was routine until we reached the ATV store. Eddie and his wife, Pat, ran the family-operated business. Inside are not only four wheelers and equipment, but also two brown Doberman pinschers. They were kept in the office and we had encountered them only twice.

Eddie also owned a cockatoo named Rosie. Up until this particular day I had only seen her through the window. Perhaps because it was race week, Eddie had her perch outside. Things got a little crazy around Bristol during race week.

As Gracie and I approached, Eddie put Rosie on his arm and proudly displayed her. Surprising me, he placed her on my arm. She sat contentedly while Gracie watched. Before I knew it, Eddie was in the shop and Rosie was crawling up my arm to nestle against my face and neck. Sweet bird, I thought.

Rosie became more curious and attempted to remove my sunglasses. I wondered what would happen next. Her beak was curved and came to a very sharp point. It looked like a camera moment to me . . . "Gracie meets Rosie." I put Rosie back on her perch so I could prepare my cell phone camera.

I then extended my forearm to Rosie, inviting her to come aboard. I felt a strong bite on the top of my hand. Ouch! Rosie! I had two puncture wounds, one from the top beak and one from the lower beak. They were about one inch apart.

Pat and Eddie came to my rescue. Pat doctored my wounds while Eddie had Rosie show me all of her tricks. I think I had seen enough of her tricks!

As we walked away Rosie said, "Come back." No thanks. I might have been breakfast, but I wasn't going to be lunch, too!

Two band-aids could not contain the blood flow. We continued our walk, delivering something to our friend Lowell's home. He gave Gracie fresh water and introduced me to his wife, Nell.

Leaving Lowell's house, we headed back to the car. We stopped at the jeweler's to speak with John the about rebuilding some of my ill-fated jewelry. By now my hand was swollen and blue. I looked at the thin skin on my left hand and observed that the veins seemed to be just underneath the surface. I began to wonder if Rosie had nicked a vein when she had bitten my right hand.

I called the animal hospital for advice. They suggested that I wash it thoroughly and keep an eye on it. The blueness and swelling continued.

Because I had formerly worked at the hospital, I knew several radiologists. I called our local hospital to ask who was working. I was told Dr. Becker was there. Dr. Becker, a fellow avid snow skier, was my friend and he had allowed me to use his dock to kayak on Watauga Lake. I asked to be transferred to the reading room.

"Wound treatment is not my specialty, but if you'll come to the circle driveway in front of the hospital, I will be glad to take a look at it for you. You won't even have to get out of the car." Great! A drive-by doctor with no charge. What a perfect idea! This could be the start of a whole new medical treatment method!

When I arrived at my car, I put fresh band-aids on the wounds. This cleaned up the blood. I called Dr. Becker as we arrived at the hospital. The timing was perfect. I did have to get out of the car because the bite was on my right hand. After he carefully examined my hand and listened to my detailed explanation of how I had been bitten by a cockatoo, Dr. Becker recommended that I use ice for the swelling and watch the wounds closely for signs of infection. Eternal thanks to Dr. Becker for his kindness!

Our destination was home. Because my hand was swelling and had two puncture marks, the bite looked like a snakebite. Easing Larry's mind, I informed him that I had seen a doctor and relayed his recommendations.

The rest of Thursday was really very nice. We had a wonderful lunch at a local restaurant and shopped for a digital camera.

Friday

Friday was a very calm day. The Happy Valley football team crushed Unaka 39–0. I guess it was my day to rest.

Saturday

Before Gracie and I left for our morning walk, I went outside to feed the wild critters. I found that the area had been autographed with footprints, large footprints. Just as we had suspected, it was a bear. Actually, it was a large bear. The front pads were three-and-a-half inches long and rear pads measured six-and-a-half inches. This did not include the long claw marks, which had left scratch marks on the concrete.

OK, no more corn for anyone. While I would have loved to have seen the bear, I decided that we really did not need it in our yard. Our carport was only about thirty feet from a densely wooded area.

A discussion with my friend Robbie helped me to figure out who had left poopers in the concrete hands that served as the bird feeder . . . it had been the bear. I really had not intended for the feeder to be used as a toilet.

At this time our oak tree was absolutely full of acorns that would continue to fall over the next few weeks. We kept a close watch on Gracie when she went outside. We did find several other scratch marks on rocks near our home. Apparently the bear had chosen to come at night when Gracie was inside. Although Gracie sniffed the area thoroughly, we had no more close encounters of the bear kind.

I had no idea who had won the car race. We'd had a full week of our own entertainment!

Grace in Your Face

With a little encouragement and a loose hold on her leash, just about anyone can experience Grace in your face. Everyone we intersect with on our walk is a potential "face off." When approaching someone, Gracie would stop and wait to see if there is interest.

Gracie never met a stranger. As folks stopped to pet her, I kept a tight hold on the leash, lest she become airborne and plant kisses on their lips. That's what she was really after. Attention was good and petting was appreciated, but a kiss on the lips was divine!

Men with beards are Gracie's prime targets. Perhaps they taste better. Maybe she was smart enough to figure out that a greater percentage of them would let her kiss them on the face. Nothing delighted her more than a face-to-face encounter.

Face to face. It's close. It's intimate. It's all out and exciting. It's the time she gave herself totally . . . no sneaking up from behind, or tiptoeing through the tulips.

Look out, world, it's Grace in your face!

Grace for the day, every situation, every decision
In every lonely place of the heart.
And every step we take.
His grace is always and will always be what carries us.
One day everything here on earth will be put in perspective and we will
soar eternally with Him!

Christmas Kisses

It was 4:00 p.m. on Christmas Eve. Gracie and I were in the car returning from a visit and exercise session with brother Rocky. We were expecting company to arrive at 4:30. At the intersection of "malfunction junction," I looked in my rearview mirror.

Glancing into another car, I saw a face that looked familiar . . . it looked like Vicki. Vicki was my friend Debbie's cousin. I remembered that Vicki's husband had just passed away a few months ago. I recognized the car and figured that she was going to the cemetery.

Sometimes you know that there are more important things in life than being on time. I drove up the hill and made a left turn into the cemetery. Proceeding to Ricky Paul's grave, I waited. Vicki was not far behind us. I put Gracie's leash on and let her get out of the car.

Much to Vicki's surprise, she was greeted by Gracie's wagging bobble (actually it was her entire rear end) and a tongue to match. Gracie sensed the mood at that moment and bathed Vicki with her very best Christmas kisses.

"You just don't know how much I needed that," Vicki told me.

Somehow the love from those deep eyes and slurpy kisses made this Christmas a little easier for Vicki. And somehow I wasn't late or even rushed to greet our company.

Dogs make such perfect messengers.
What they deliver is often sent from above!

The Python and the
Broken Pedestal

Arriving home from a morning walk, I discovered that we had a leak in the hot tub. As Larry and I removed the panels, I quickly discovered the source of the leak. As we got down on our hands and knees to examine the problem, we each received a good dose of Grace in the face. Our efforts to tighten the hose clamps accentuated the problem. The drip soon became water spewing. Working to divert the water, we used a ten-foot-long plastic drainage pipe that had been on the deck for a year.

Larry carefully rigged the pipe to a funnel and used it to channel the water away from the deck. Suddenly this pipe came to life and Gracie sprang into action. Her determined barking alerted the neighborhood to the presence of danger.

Living on the edge of the woods, we had dealt with our share of snakes. Heidi and Gina Marie had earned "Red Hearts" and my eternal thanks when they had alerted me to a black snake in our basement. Grace seemed to live above them and had never noticed the time there was a five-foot-long black snake lying against our back porch. It was Larry who had escorted it to the woods.

Back to the python. Apparently the "python" had been barked at before and knew how to play dead. No amount of canine vocalization could get it to budge. Just about the time Larry finished precariously balancing it in place, Gracie summoned her courage and pounced on the python. Pleased with her hunting capabilities, she dragged it into the yard, proudly displaying her catch.

Kill . . . no, I never actually considered it. I was thinking more along the lines of a one-way trip to Jupiter, Mars, or Uranus. Pluto seemed more in line with her personality. By now she was in full dress Mama Molly mode. I armed myself with a stick as she taunted me with the doggie favorite, "Catch me if you can, and we both know that you can't!" This lasted long enough to fill her with delight and I was able to grab her collar.

Into the basement we marched. The muddy paws required eight sheets of baby wipes before they were clean. It was then that I began to wonder if the Russians needed another dog in space. By the time she returned, all would be forgiven.

When Gracie falls off the pedestal of good behavior, the whole pedestal comes crashing down. Never let it be said that she is perfect. But that's why Grace came. It brought hope to the imperfect. Much as she loves us, every now and then the "Mollyodic nature" surfaces.

It's all about Grace
By Grace we made it through yesterday
By Grace we will live victoriously today
By Grace we have hope for tomorrow
By Grace we live eternity!

Double Agent

It was a very hot, sultry July day. We cut our morning walk a little short and returned to the car. As I reached for the door, I discovered a note attached. "Miss Susan, Kathy left her drama script at the church last night. Can you help? Thanks. Jennifer." Sure, we could swing by the church and pick up the script.

As I entered the church, I noticed that the floor needed cleaning. Vacation Bible school was in full swing as children were discovering The Rock of Ages. Sister Pat stopped by to deliver more prizes for Miss Kathy's General Store. Gracie was thrilled to meet a new friend. This was no ordinary friend; this was a friend with toys! As Pat and I examined each prize, Gracie's excitement grew. Pat pulled a plastic "duck bill" from the prizes. It was on a string and if you blew into it just right, a loud quack was sounded. "That's just what I need," I said. "By the end of Vacation Bible School, my voice resembles Minnie Mouse's tiniest baby. I need an attention-getter." We left all the items in the bags for Miss Kathy to place in the General Store.

Pat blessed me tremendously, as she volunteered to help clean the church. She was busy cleaning the bathrooms while I vacuumed. Gracie had other things on her mind. She disappeared into the General Store. This could get interesting. The store was filled with dolls, stuffed animals, balls, and other assorted treasures. She had already chosen a tennis ball, chewed it in half, and had begun to strip the cover off. That wound up in the garbage can. Another lightweight plastic ball lay squashed on the floor. Balls were one of her specialties. Stuffed animals rated highly, too.

Emerging from the General Store, she held in her mouth the plastic bag containing the duck bill. It was even the color I had wanted. She graciously allowed me to take it and place it in my pocket. Every now and then, her perception amazed me.

My Lord surprises me sometimes by the way He meets my needs. Sister Pat was His agent today, and every now and then Gracie was His agent. Thank you, Lord, for double agents!

Prayer Dog

When she was about seven years old, Gracie had a benign growth removed from the outside of her ankle. We had to watch her very closely so she would not lick the area. It healed well until the stitches were taken out. The wound was on the bend of her ankle and, without stitches to hold it together, it popped open.

Dr. Kapoor closed the area with staples this time. Again, we were on guard, watching her almost every minute. Finally, the day came for the staples to come out. Whew! We made it. The celebration was short lived as it opened up again.

The third attempt to close the wound required making a new incision and stitching it closed. This seemed to work great until the stitches were removed. Once again, it opened up. We had to let it close gradually, which left a larger scar, but eventually it did heal.

During this time of faithfully watching her, I kept Gracie with me as much as I could. She went with me to Friday morning intercessory prayer time. It was summer, so we were meeting at the gazebo on the Doe River across from First Freewill Baptist Church in Elizabethton. Gracie actually seemed to enjoy the time spent in prayer and was very well behaved. I had taught her to "say her prayers" by placing both paws on my leg while I was kneeling down and she was in a sitting position.

During prayer time she also got to meet Doris and spend some time with Carla. She was the "WATCH DOG" for the Watchmen on the Walls intercessory prayer group. She certainly kept the neighborhood cats at bay. The squirrels appreciated that. It had not been too long ago when one of the cats had captured a squirrel. I had sprung into action and demanded it release the victim. My outrage had even surprised Carla and Doris. It had worked, as the cat had dropped his prey and the squirrel had been able to escape.

Gracie was used to the blowing of the shofar. The instrument fascinated her because it was a ram's horn. This sent her "nose and noise alarm" off and her not so secret desire was to chew on it!

Walking By Grace

I believe that Gracie's favorite time of day is our morning walk. We have made so many friends and she has brightened many days just delivering love and grace.

When Gracie was a puppy, I was working an early shift at the hospital. We would wake up at 4:30 a.m. and take our walk at about 5:15 a.m. We walked in the parking lot of a local school. I already knew the custodians who came in early to open the school. Gracie was delighted to visit Gloria and Jena each morning. This was before the days of such tight security in schools and we were allowed to go inside their office and say good morning. Gloria and Jena were both animal lovers and showered their kindness on Gracie. Occasionally, Gracie would ride in Gloria's big truck. She really never did drive it.

The biology teacher, Mr. Wheels, came in early, too. Gracie knew exactly which classroom was his and visited regularly. She discovered chewing gum underneath the desktops and loved to give Mr. Wheels her sloppy kisses.

On days that I did not work, we established a walking route that included many other visitors who quickly became Gracie's admirers.

Jan worked at a local cell phone store. Gracie would look through the window for Jan's curly blonde hair. Jan had several dogs of her own and Gracie brightened her day. In time, the business became so successful that a larger building was needed. The floor was laminate and Gracie's toenails made a clicking noise that resembled tap dancing. Doug, Stephen, Matt, and Meagan now worked with Jan at the store and welcomed Gracie into their day and lives.

Jan quickly became my technical assistant. Being "electronically challenged," I counted on Jan to pull me through many cell phone crises. The day I dropped my phone in the washing machine, she was able to give me advice on how to revive it again. About six weeks later, I put the phone through an entire wash cycle. This proved to be fatal and Jan found a good used phone to replace it.

The next stop on our walks was the Express Care store owned by Greg. The entire staff there looked forward to Gracie's morning visits. Karen and Amy provided treats. Mike, Robbie, Bobby, Wade, Phillip, and Keith were always glad to see her. Keith made the mistake of getting down in the "play" or challenge position and Gracie never forgot that. "Oh, Keith," I explained, "You just can't do that with Gracie." Since Gracie had a roughneck side or sides, we did our best to not encourage this type of human interaction. She loved it and did not know when to quit. She never forgot Keith's invitation to play, and every time she saw him, she was ready to pounce!

Judy and Jessica at the money-lending store joined the Gracie fan club. Judy purchased treats for Gracie. For security reasons, Judy and Jessica worked behind glass windows. Gracie would come into the store, throw her big paws up on the counter, and beg for the treats. Judy carefully passed them through the opening in the window. Occasionally, the girls would come out of their enclosures and visit with Gracie. Gracie was glad to perform her tricks when she was rewarded with treats. Margaret was present some days. Being a fellow boxer owner, she enjoyed Gracie, too.

Many of the folks at the grocery store got to know Gracie as well. As they collected carts or we passed by the door, Gracie would peer in. I'm sure she would have loved to work in the meat department, but that just never worked out. Amy and her mom, Diane, would go out of their way to see Gracie. Diane drove Amy to work many days and always looked for Gracie and me as we walked. Tracy, John, Karen, Eddie, Shirley, and Jeff all became members of the Gracie fan club. She was always delighted to see them, too!

The next stop was the card shop. The girls who worked there provided Gracie with treats. She knew exactly where they were stored and went through her routine of tricks to receive her goodies. On October 31 I would dress her in a doggie skeleton costume, which produced many smiles from the regulars on our walk and turned lots of heads as people drove by.

We became good customers at the card shop. I would shop while Gracie visited. I discovered the half-price corner and found many bargains there!

Jackie, Carol, Margie, Bethany, Ann, and Linda all looked forward to our daily visits almost as much as Gracie did!

The sports store was the next treat dispenser. I kept a bag of treats under the counter and she went right to them. Ryan, Alex, Joe, Kathy, Preston, Malila, Madison, Sam, Theresa, and Nathaniel came to know Gracie. I found lots of bargains on the markdown racks. Larry teased me, saying, "You can't even walk a dog without shopping." It was true!

Gracie was the first customer at the new pet store. She walked the aisles before they were stocked. There was always a container of treats available. Sheila, Baylie, Helena, and Fred were her favorite people to greet.

The drive-through window at a local bank proved to be another good place to find treats. The employees enjoyed Gracie's visits. When the window was busy, we would use the lane that had what we called "rocket ship delivery." Her treat was placed within a plastic container that ran through a tube. We met many wonderful employees there, including Angie, Joy, Meagen, Judy, Samantha, and Betty.

One more bank completed the visiting/treat circuit. It all started with Paulette, who I went to church with. She worked the drive-through window and loved to see Gracie. After Paulette retired, Kim assumed command of the drive-through treat window and provided Gracie with green treats, her favorite. Melissa, Cindy, Marie, Patty, and Brittany worked inside the bank.

Gracie was becoming Elizabethton's canine social queen. Whenever she saw a person, she would stop and wait. She fully expected that they would come and visit her. She delivered lots of love, affection, and encouragement to folks along the way. I remember one man's comment:

"Now that is a magnificent piece"

He was right. She was strikingly beautiful. Her white socks and abundance of flash (white fur) accentuated the brindle stripes. Boxer lovers driving by would often stop and talk to us. We shared our boxer stories as Gracie shared her love.

Friends of Grace

Occasionally, we would stop by to visit our local jeweler, John. John was always glad to set his work aside for a few minutes to greet Gracie. She simply could never get enough attention. Ann, Anna, and Joan worked with John and welcomed Gracie's visits, too.

I belonged to a local women's fitness center for a couple of years. Brenda owned the business and was one of Gracie's favorites. Brenda often had some type of goodie to share with Gracie. Perhaps this had something to do with Brenda being so high up on Gracie's list! Brenda's friend, Monique, worked nearby and visited Gracie often. Many times, we made the trip to see her at the insurance office. Gracie just had a way of brightening people's day. No matter what someone was going through, Gracie brought sunshine and joy. I often called her my sunshine girl. When Grace came into a place, everything changed!

So many ladies got to know Gracie. I was known to many as "Gracie's mom." As friendly as Gracie was to everyone, she had a peculiar behavior when she was left alone in the car. I left the windows cracked open for fresh air while she sat inside. She was very well behaved and would sit and watch for my return. If someone approached her as she sat in the car, she would turn her head and not even look at them. This seemed so out of character given her friendly nature. I suppose that when she was left in the car, she was on constant patrol as she awaited my return and could not be distracted.

Whenever we had repairs done inside our home, Gracie greeted the workers with delight. She absolutely loved the drain doctors, Marvin, Jimmy, Shane, Scotty, and J.T. They were down on her level as they worked on plumbing problems. These guys knew how to receive her enthusiasm and wet, sloppy kisses. We ran into them many times either at the bank or our local home improvement store. I'm not sure who was more entertaining, Gracie or the guys.

"When you love and accept someone who belongs to me,
You love and accept me."
Brenda

Downtown Elizabethton

When the weather was hot and sunny or perhaps threatening rain, Gracie and I took walks in downtown Elizabethton. For those not from East Tennessee, the proper pronunciation is E-liz-a-BETH-ton. Visitors attempt to put the accent on "ton". This is a mouthful and quite difficult to say. The covered walkways of the downtown area provide shelter from the elements. It was a treat for me to window shop, as there are many interesting shops. Quite often I would do more than just window shop!

Elizabethton has many small businesses and antique shops. I was never really interested in antiques until I became one myself. Shopping in an antique store now is like visiting my childhood home!

The local coffee shop, owned by John and Lisa, frequently supplied Gracie with a bowl of cold water. A young man named Will provided "walk up" service when I ordered a mocha fit frappe. You just can't beat that! Two German ladies, Irene and Uschi, prepared the wonderful food and took a special liking to Gracie as they watched her through the windows.

My friend Kathy owns a business in town and looked forward to Gracie and I coming. This gave us an opportunity to catch up on news and share the goodness of God with one another.

The sporting goods store downtown welcomed Gracie's visits, too. Ray always made us feel welcome.

Across the street from Ray's shop is a hardware store that is over one hundred years old. The wooden floors creak a little, and I can't help but wonder what it was like to shop inside those walls many years ago. The store is a valuable piece of Elizabethton's history. Here you will find yesterday's treasures, such as a red wagon, pottery, galvanized washtubs and tools, as well as today's supplies. The gentleman who owns the store enjoyed seeing Gracie, too. He shared many stories of yesteryear with me. His daughter now helps in the store and we swapped "boxer stories," as she owns a boxer named Penny. Although the store is not open every day, shopping there is like stepping back in time.

Yates Remnant Shop has been in Elizabethton since September of 1962. Founder, Pauline Yates, stocked a wide variety of fabrics. Her daughter, Kay, currently runs the store. Employees Bernice, Gladys, Eunice, Juanita, Pauline, Gail, and Debbie have probably all waited on me down through the years. Rebekah keeps the window displays looking good. Gracie was usually well behaved in this store as I chose the right fabric for my next project. I always felt welcomed, knowing that Gracie was welcomed too!

Gracie delighted in the lovely park downtown, cooled her feet in the Doe River, and even liked to stroll through the historic covered bridge. Many ducks and geese swam peacefully in the river, and we did our best to give them space. After all, we were in their territory. Although it is the nature of a dog to chase other critters, I did my best to teach Gracie to respect their lives, too.

I was always careful to keep Gracie close to me, as I realized that not everyone was comfortable around dogs. For those who welcomed her, she gave lots of love in return. Gracie had a special gift of making people feel special and accepted. She carried and delivered grace to those who were willing to receive it. What a blessing it is to carry grace to others!

Santa and Me

When I was a child, my parents took us to visit Santa Claus so that we could present our list of requested gifts. There was just nothing like being on Santa's lap and knowing that he cared and would bring me whatever I asked for. Well, he didn't bring me everything I wanted. I had long lists!

Santa was scheduled to appear at our local farm and tractor supply store. His mission was to pose for photographs with pets. This was a fundraiser for a low-cost spay/neuter clinic. It was actually Charli who suggested that we take Bear and Gracie.

Although Gracie dearly loved people, there were very few dogs that she reacted well to. I knew that there would be a lot of dogs and cats present and I really did not look forward to the event.

Armed with a strong leash, I decided to brave the event. Santa was late and the line was long. Bear and Gracie did well together. Many dogs kept their distance from Gracie, but Hobo decided he wanted to meet her. Hobo belonged to Dave, one of the employees at the store.

Hobo had been adopted as a puppy. Dave had been told Hobo was a beagle. Hobo turned out to be the biggest "beagle" Dave had ever seen. He was actually closer to Gracie's size. He was a brave, strong dog who had protected his family and property by killing two coyotes that had threatened the family's safety.

Hobo was in line behind us. Dave and I decided that we would give it a go and let the pups get to know each other. Hobo and Gracie sniffed each other. This is the get acquainted formula in "doggiedom." Stage one of the getting to know you went well. Gracie and Hobo backed off and looked at each other. Gracie spoke first. "Ruff ruff ruff ruff ruff." Hobo took off and ran like the wind.

Dave could not believe that his macho dog was so intimidated by Gracie. She had to be the boss!

We were finally able to get the photographs with Santa made. Gracie loved Santa and all the fine employees at the store. Whitney, Tommy, Scott, Tonya, Hannah, Jaime, and Molly worked with Dave. Gracie's favorite employee was whoever was working the cash register. She knew that the treats were located behind the counter and freely begged for them.

Christmas Biscuits

Sunday morning walks are a little different. Most of the stores are closed. Last Sunday we were walking by the car wash and our path intersected with the path of a man who lived in the neighborhood. Lowell always had time for a Gracie greeting. Today he explained that his neighbor had a dog named Foxy who looked just like Gracie. He cheerfully related to me that on Christmas day he had baked biscuits and had made some gravy. He had shared them with Foxy. Apparently the biscuits had not exactly been Betty Crocker quality. He described them as having been flat and hard. Foxy, on the other hand, had loved them and had been most grateful.

When measured by appearance, the biscuits had been a flop. Many would have discarded them and tried again. Foxy had looked beyond their appearance and had found flavor, goodness, and a gift given in love with pure motives. Her excitement and pleasure had brought joy to Lowell.

Dogs seem to have a unique ability to cut through the fluff and respond in a genuine way. They simply do not judge. Appearance and presentation could never take the place of a gift given from a heart of love.

Lowell became a regular Sunday morning walking buddy. When Gracie saw him coming (or I should say we, because I was on the other end of the leash), Gracie bolted across the parking lot to greet him. Gracie quickly had him trained. She would sit, shake, say her prayers, and then give him a big boxer hug, which included a face washing. Performing her tricks, she learned he would give her anything . . . even before he gave the commands. On birthdays or Christmas he gave her presents. Many of these became her favorites.

Many times I heard people say
"Thank you for stopping. She made my day!"
Gracie, the Daymaker!

Smitten

This morning we took a leisurely walk through charming and historic downtown Elizabethton. It was still quite early, so most of the businesses had not opened yet.

Gracie loved Elizabethton. The covered walks provided shelter on a rainy day or relief from the hot sunshine. Several of the merchants knew her by name and enjoyed her visits. Gracie found many interesting sights and smells in the park area, the covered bridge, and Doe River.

Today, in front of the Coffee Company, we spotted a truck parked. Sitting in the passenger's seat was a handsome retriever. I cannot say whether she caught his scent first or saw him. As Gracie stopped to look, I held her leash tightly. I had played this game before . . . she would sniff the other dog, then someone would get a little growly and then it would get ugly. This time was different.

Perhaps it was his size. He easily outweighed her by fifty pounds. Maybe it was his aura of strength and confidence. She paused and their eyes met. The look on his face said it all. Eyes half closed, relaxed, and enthralled, he definitely liked what he saw. If dogs are capable of love at first sight, this was it.

About that time, his owner exited the truck from the street side. "I think we have two new members for the mutual admiration society," I said to myself.

"I don't understand it," his owner explained. "He usually barks and carries on when he sees another dog." From the look on his face, I really didn't think that he wanted to intimidate her. It must have been animal magnetism. Gracie was acting out of character, too. She was content to look and enjoy his presence.

I'm sure that if we had allowed them to meet, it would have been an interesting introduction. His owner was on the way to an appointment, though. Gracie's Mr. Dreamboat was a therapy dog and he visited terminally ill patients. Good choice, Gracie!

Mulch Mountain

This morning's walk presented a new challenge for Gracie and some insight for me. We were strolling along in front of Elizabethton High School when Gracie suddenly stopped. She saw something that made her fearful. All sixteen feet of her retractable leash were fully extended as she circled an area of shrubbery and flowers. "What is it, girl?" I asked, searching for the cause of her fear. Whatever "it" was, she wanted no part of it. Steer clear and watch your backside!

Not knowing what to expect, I made her stop so I could examine the area closely. I almost laughed when I found the cause for alarm. Someone had placed an extremely frightening pile of mulch in her path. The mountain of mulch was perhaps two feet tall and maybe three feet across. I never knew that mulch could be so intimidating.

What was totally harmless to me, because I knew what it was, produced fear and apprehension in Gracie. It was an unwelcomed change. It had not been there yesterday and therefore it could not be trusted.

My first instinct was to avoid the intruder. My second and prevailing idea was to teach her that she did not need to fear Mulch Mountain. It's not like she hadn't seen mulch before. One hundred feet away from us was a real mulch mountain, which stood fifteen feet high and thirty feet across. She loved to sink her feet into that mulch.

I gently led her to the small pile of mulch. Once she became convinced that it was not threatening, we began to move closer to the object of her fear. On our third approach, her courage and curiosity overcame her fear. She had faced her fear and gained victory over it. She was free to continue our walk, unhampered by fear.

My mind quickly turned to the destructive power of fear. When it dominates, faith flounders. Or is it better said that when faith flounders, fear dominates? Fear causes us to get off track, to draw back, to hesitate. It opens up inroads of doubt and mistrust. Fear oppresses and dominates. It has power to control our thinking and actions.

I had no fear of the mulch because I knew the truth about it. To Gracie, it was a change that she did not understand and therefore it threatened her security. Once she realized the truth, she was set free from her fear. I determined in my heart to know truth and not walk in fear.

You shall know the truth and the truth shall set you free!
John 8:32

Merrily We Roll Along

Bobby is one of the few people who will allow Gracie to lavish her love on his face. He also shares his breakfast with her. You just can't beat a friend like that!

It was a slow morning at the express lube store. Bobby was seated on an office chair that had wheels on it. Gracie seized the opportunity to give Bobby one of her "Gracie hugs." As she wrapped her paws around him, the chair began to roll backwards. This challenged her desire to remain close and she took two steps closer, trying to keep up with the rolling chair.

The dance continued until she backed him into a filing cabinet. The game was over, but the love continued.

To a boxer, it's all about fun or people or fun or eating or fun or sleeping or just plain fun. Life is just too short to be taken seriously!

Luv 'em, Lick em's Part Two

Behind her rough and tumble exterior, there lies a sensitivity in Gracie that astounds me. She seems to be able to connect with the deep needs of people.

Today was just such an example. Undaunted by the light rain falling, Gracie walked on and noticed everything and everybody. As we approached the automatic door of the grocery store, an older man and his grown daughter exited. I stopped short and held Gracie to make room for them.

"It's OK," said the young lady. "May I pet her?" Not wanting to overwhelm her with Gracie's typical enthusiasm and face washing, I held her at bay while the young lady stroked her head. I took note that Gracie was drawn to the woman and ignored the gentleman. This was unusual, as Gracie preferred men.

By now, Gracie was gaining momentum and the exchange between the two was growing. "You can put your paws on me," our new friend said. With that permission, the official Gracie greeting was set in motion. Up came the paws, which rested on the woman's chest, and out came the tongue, which seemed to grow with every lick Gracie gave.

Our new friends obviously did not have many of this world's riches. That made absolutely no difference to Gracie . . . there was a very touching heart-to-heart exchange occurring. Somehow, Gracie just sensed that her new friend needed love.

I understood as the daughter began to share that their dog had been shot and killed just five days before. Her heart was in need of the unconditional love that dogs are such experts at dispensing. The daughter's face began to brighten as Gracie's attention made her feel so special and loved again.

As we tried to part ways, Gracie moved toward her, repeating the exchange of affection. It was a beautiful display of complete acceptance.

As we resumed our walk, I marveled at God's timing. If we had arrived fifteen seconds earlier or later, we would have missed the moment. The opportunity to impart love to others usually doesn't come on our precise timetable, but it does come. Gracie had been ready. She had sensed the need and had been available to brighten someone's day.

May we carry the sensitivity of grace,

And

Take the time

To deliver it to those who need it.

Licorice Socks

Our Monday morning walk was in Elizabethton and we walked along the Doe River. I took time to pick up aluminum cans and plastic litter. It seemed that Gracie's antenna detected multi-tasking. This activated the "ACTING OUT" button.

I bent over to retrieve a bottle from the edge of Mill Race. This was her cue to head for the water. Her seventy-pound frame sank into the rich black mud, which resembled quick sand. Quick mud was what I decided to call it. Her beautiful white anklets were now licorice colored. The feel of mud between her toes sent Gracie into a trapezoidian run. Remember, she was on a sixteen-foot leash, and I was connected to the other end.

I felt like a bullfighter as her licorice feet thundered toward me. My biggest concern was a collision that would send me sprawling with black paw prints all over me. She ran in circles around me and I was able to keep distance between us. Somehow, I was able to dodge her advances. The game continued until the "grazillas" tired out and she calmed down.

We then had a foot washing service at the river. I won't say they were spotless, but it was a vast improvement over licorice socks!

Pokey Joe

Jumping out of the car was always exciting. Gracie knew that great adventures and her special friends, sights, smells, and sounds, awaited us.

Getting back into the car after our outing was another story. Unless there was a downpour, she never seemed to be ready. Approaching the car, I pressed the remote "unlock" button. She had learned that this was her cue. Hearing the click, she would frequently just stop in her tracks, refusing to go further.

What would an observer see? A woman behind a seventy-pound boxer, pushing its rear end in the direction of the car. Stubborn? Strong-willed? What can I say? I have been accused of those characteristics myself! While Gracie may not win the battle, she always makes her point. . . . "I'm not ready to go yet. There is still more fun to be had."

Led By Grace

Most of our walks were led by me. Somehow I managed to keep control of my frisky walking companion.

Every now and then, Gracie exhibited an unusual interest in going another direction. Today was one of those days. We were walking by a building that houses a local agency to help the poor. They distribute food, clothing, and toys—whatever is needed. Gracie had never paid any attention to the agency before today. Today, I let her take the lead.

She walked up to the door and peered in. A face like Gracie's always caused excitement. I was told to bring her in and let her look around as long as she did not get around the food. Once inside, we found lots of workers who ogled over Gracie. Of course, she loved the attention.

As I looked around, I saw several original oil paintings. I immediately focused on a painting of an eagle ready to land on her nest, which contained three eggs. I inquired if I could purchase the painting. I suggested that the money be used as a donation to help support the ministry. The person in charge replied that I could not purchase the painting, but that the artist could give it to me.

The artist quickly introduced himself. He was a retired surgeon who took mission trips to Africa to share his faith. He brought his paintings to the agency to bless the needy. We shared our faith and he blessed me with the eagle painting.

The eagle is such a majestic bird. Its ability to soar has spoken volumes to me as I learn to navigate above circumstances.

This eagle was not soaring. She was preparing to rest on the nest and wait for her eggs to hatch. At that time I had been caring for two loved ones who were in the hospital. I had been doing a lot of sitting and waiting. The Lord spoke to my heart and said, "If you don't sit on the eggs, they will never hatch."

I love to soar, but sometimes I need to sit on the nest and wait. He assured me that my eggs would hatch.

I love being led by Grace!

Grace Walk, Ouch!

The linear park in Erwin has a beautiful four-and-a-half mile paved trail. When I first biked it a couple of years ago, I knew it would be a Gracie place. Today was her day.

The twenty-minute drive was relaxing. The leaves were beginning to change colors and the sky was a clear blue so typical of autumn in upper East Tennessee. Arriving at the park, I opened the back hatch of my car and attached Gracie's leash. Gracie could tell that this was no ordinary walk.

The sights and smells on the trail were new, exciting, and intriguing. If Grace could talk, I'm sure I would have heard about every doggie scent that tickled her nostrils. Her enthusiasm forced me to walk at a faster pace. With no people around, this was pure doggie adventure.

Indian Creek provided a great place for Gracie to cool her toes. The pleasant sound of water gushing over and around rocks was peaceful and serene. I carried some old bread to feed the ducks. As we reached the bridge, they gathered below, waiting for breakfast. Gracie watched, looking through the rails as Romeo and Juliet (two large white ducks) were joined by several mallards, wood ducks, and an unusual black and white duck that appeared to have eyeliner around its eyes. Gracie preferred to keep moving, but she waited patiently while I emptied the bread bag.

Our return trip on the trail was just as exciting to Gracie. When I stopped to sit on a bench, she jumped right up and sat next to me. As we continued our journey, she decided it was time to play "snatch the leash." It's all in good fun. The game required only two participants. The first was a dog who wanted control of the leash. Gracie accomplished this by grabbing the leash in her mouth and running with it. Apparently it was fair to growl playfully and grab at the human's sleeves.

We'd played this game before. It could be subtitled "Who's walking who?" There was no clear winner.

Eventually the game came to a standstill and we resumed our normal walk. Investigating a scent, Gracie stepped off the trail. She picked up her left rear foot and tried to shake something off of it. Putting weight on her foot again caused her to limp and then shake the foot harder.

I stopped to check her pads. I found a large thorn embedded in her pad and removed it easily. She continued on our brisk walk with no limp and no thought of what the problem had been.

How simple. How easy. A thorn in the flesh. It was painful. It was intruding and hindering her walk. Could she have removed it herself? We'll never know, because she has a master who saw her leave the trail and knew right away that she had a problem. Her master cared. Her master stopped. Her master easily removed the thorn and she just kept on walking.

The thorns of life are out there. We are going to step on them every now and then. They hurt and make our walk uncomfortable. We would be wise to just stop and let the Master remove what is painful and then keep walking. We don't have to figure everything out and have an answer for it all. The Master knows, cares, and heals.

She is My Defense

One of my favorite songs is "He is my Defense." Today Gracie served as His agent, my defender.

Gracie was usually a people magnet. Young, old, rich, poor . . . everyone who liked dogs was drawn to Gracie. At least, until today.

As Gracie and I were waiting for my car to be repaired, we took a walk in an area of town that was probably not the safest place to be. It was quite early in the morning and very few people were up and about. My mechanic advised me to stay on the main road. Gracie enjoyed the change of scenery, new smells, and different sounds. I kept her close to me, as there was more traffic than she was used to.

Keeping my focus forward, I saw three very large men on the sidewalk about two blocks ahead of us. Their appearance concerned me and I considered crossing the street to avoid confrontation. Not one to be driven by fear, I prayed, "Lord, let them see Your protection over me." I envisioned that they would see huge angels towering over us. Two of the men began to take a detour, avoiding us. By the time we reached the third man, the other two were a block away.

The third man was about twice my size. I pulled Gracie close to me. He stepped off the curb to walk in the street. "What's your dog's name?" he asked and took a step backwards.

"Gracie," I replied. He took another step backward into the street.

"What kind of dog is she?" was his next question.

"She's a boxer." Continuing his retreat, he gestured with his hands that he wanted nothing to do with a boxer. Works for me!

As we walked on, I knew my prayers had been answered. The men had seen my protection. She was my defense and I would not be moved. To get to me, you had to get past my protection. Nobody did it better!

Choices

We all make choices every day. Some of them are really insignificant decisions. . . . Some are life changing. What a wonderful gift God gave us, the ability to make choices.

Gracie rarely gets to makes her own choices. Her master (i.e. me. Gracie, are you listening?) decides what time we go walking, where we go, how long we are gone. The Master leads and the canine follows.

Today it was a sweet treat to see Gracie make some choices. We arrived at our local paint store to decide what color to paint the deck and the bridge that spans our tiny creek. I knew I wanted dark brown, but I had a hard time choosing between two shades. Plantation brown was lighter and chateau brown darker. I laid the two sample swatches on the counter and decided on the lighter of the two.

"Let's let Gracie choose," I told Andy who was helping me. Again, I laid the swatches down. Gracie raised herself by placing her front paws on the counter to get a better look. She slapped her left paw down on the planta-tion brown swatch. "That's it," I said. Then I remembered that plantation brown was the color of our original trim work and shutters when our home was built in 1976.

Just for interest, we decided to give her another choice. We laid three samples down, rearranging the colors. When asked to choose, she clearly landed her big white paw on plantation brown again.

That was it! We ordered the paint and headed for a park in Elizabethton for our morning walk. There, we intersected with Jennie, who was visiting from Albuquerque. Gracie never met a stranger and gladly welcomed Jennie to "her" park. Jennie was in our area for several days on what she called "an adventure."

Jennie was graciously given the official kisses and affection patented by Elizabeth Grace. We shared about the area and gave her directions to Wilbur Dam and Watauga Lake. "While you are in town, you need to check out at least two stores. Barnes-Boring, which is over one hundred years old, and the Three Ladies Craft and Gift Shop where local crafters sell their work." We offered to walk with her.

Gracie always enjoys seeing the gentlemen who owns Barnes-Boring. His kindness and gentle nature are evident to all. Three Ladies has been a favorite ever since Gracie discovered "the dog room." It's not the canine clothing, or decorative carriers and purses, or even the leashes that interest her. It's not even the crate that probably reminds her of days gone by when she was confined to a crate while we were at work. It's what's on top of the crate. The nose knows. In no time that cute little white chin was resting near the bully sticks. A gentle rumble came out . . . please. . . . Jennie watched in amusement as Gracie continued her pleading. I have learned to leave my wallet in the car because I can always find something I want to purchase in this store.

Since I had no money with me, Gracie's answer was "no." Jennie, however, found her irresistible and offered to buy her a package of bully sticks. I thought it would be interesting to let her choose which package she wanted.

"Jaws" has to have the thickest, toughest bully sticks. Anything less will be devoured quickly and the last three inches must be thrown away or she will swallow it whole. I picked three packages from the "tough guy" category and allowed Gracie to choose. She was thrilled with the shopping experience and quietly chewed on the stinky bully stick as we shopped. The smaller of the two had been reduced to swallowing level by now and the larger one would be tomorrow's treat.

What a gift God gave us. The ability to choose. It's also a huge responsibility. May we have the wisdom and grace from above to choose only what our Master wants us to have.

Grace Abounds

As we walked this morning, we noticed a sparrow lying on the sidewalk. Apparently it had flown into a window and was injured. He was bright and perky and opened his beak wide as if expecting a late breakfast.

Having rescued several birds, I knew it was best to see if they could recover on their own. I picked him up, laid him on the edge of a wooded area, and prayed "Lord, if this little one can make it on his own, then let him be gone when I return. Should he need special help, allow him to be right here when I return."

We continued walking, visiting with Gracie's special friends along the way. Karen at Express Care provided a soft rag just in case I needed to cuddle the sparrow. We completed our walk and I loaded Gracie in the car. Leaving Gracie in the car freed my "leash hand" for the rescue. As I approached the woods my mind raced, wondering what I would find.

"Chirpie" was exactly where I had left him. He looked a bit disheveled, as if he had attempted to move. I reached down and gently covered him with a soft rag, taking care to keep his wings in a natural position. The process of picking him up caused excitement and a stirring of feathers. As I pulled him close to me, he settled down and began to rest. His frightened, pounding heart slowed to normal as he rested, protected by one much stronger than he.

I drove home one handed and called in reinforcements. Marissa, my twelve-year-old friend, wanted to become a veterinarian. It sounded like a perfect match. I did not need to drive my five-speed car with only one hand and Marissa needed a job. Her dad brought her over to my house and we headed for the wildlife rehabilitation center, which was twenty-two miles up Stoney Creek.

Chirpie loved to be held and grasped Marissa's finger with his tiny feet. He truly seemed to enjoy the soft cuddling. We spoke in soft tones as we traveled. Arriving at the rehabilitation center, we were told that Chirpie was an adult sparrow that had neurological injuries probably caused from flying into a window. He would be given treatment to see if he could recover.

As I reflected on Matthew 10:29–31, I remembered that Father knew Chirpie had fallen. Marissa, Gracie, and I were His agents, delivering him to a place of healing.

If God so cares for the sparrow, how much more does He care for us? It strengthened my faith to think of His all-knowing grace and love.

He who scatters sunshine will have
Light, warmth and cheer,
Even when
His sun has set.
You are here in order to
Enable the world to love more amply,
Have greater vision
And a fine spirit of hope
Which brings fulfillment
And joy!

Grace Sees

Carla, Gracie, and I had a wonderful walk on the campus of Milligan College. Gracie had become used to the large buffalo statue on campus. She never saw him move and therefore no longer felt the need to make a wide sweep around him.

As we strolled next to Buffalo Creek, Gracie received a "red alert." She was certain that something was on the other side of the water. Stopping to sniff the air, she stared intently across the creek. I glanced that way and informed Gracie that there was nothing there. Gracie knew better.

My human senses detected nothing out of place. I saw a peaceful creek, gently flowing water, no birds, ducks, geese, or cats . . . nothing. I tugged at her leash and encouraged her to move on.

Gracie saw something more. Grace always saw more than humans were able to detect. My eyes focused on a large rock across the creek. To the left of the rock, I saw a groundhog sitting perfectly still, blending in with its surroundings. I hadn't detected it at first, but Gracie had seen it clearly.

The Father's grace sees beyond what I see. He moves in a realm that works outside of my senses. Grace sees what I cannot, until I learn to operate by His Grace.

Leash Burn

Leash burn is a dog owner's version of rope burn. It occurs when a retractable leash is extended. The leash case is held in one hand and, for some unknown reason, the human grabs the extended leash in the other hand. Perhaps it was a control issue. More than likely it was a "What was I thinking?" moment.

I must have noticed a car or something, which caused me to gather the loose leash with my free hand. That was my part. It was a perfect setup for leash burn. Whatever I was attempting to keep Gracie from caused her to bolt. In a flash, the sixteen feet of leash zipped over my skin and burned the top layers of my ring finger and pinkie. Ouch! How could a leash burn?

Expecting to find abrasions, I was surprised to discover only redness. It was a lesson quickly learned.

Leash burn according to Susan: The burning action of sixteen feet of leash rushing through the fingers. Not to be repeated.

Leash burn according to Gracie: Finger burns doled out as punishment to an over-controlling mother.

Control is a hot topic in relationships—whether it's teacher/student, husband/wife, owner/dog, or parent/child. Somebody has to lead, providing safety, protection, and direction. Some of us can be led gently. Others need the rod or discipline. The more willing we are to obey, the less external control is needed. Self-control reduces the need for external control. Are you reading this, Gracie?

"We see 'him' walking you everyday"
So who is walking who?

144

Intruders

Most of our daily walks are sheer delight. This morning it was a challenge. Gracie caught a glimpse of another dog strolling along. I am very cautious of loose dogs, as I have no way to control their behavior. The dog assessed that Gracie was twice its size, and quickly changed directions. That excited Gracie even more. There must be some kind of canine rush when another animal is scared enough to run from you.

Gracie ran the length of her retractable leash as I braced for the inevitable jolt on my arm and shoulder. The impact of the jolt is magnified by the length of the leash when the jolt occurs. Having survived the impact with my arm still attached, I decided to be more aware of our surroundings and keep her closer to me. It wasn't long before Gracie spotted a woman walking her chow. This time I put the brakes on when she was five feet away from me. She pulled and strained, making both of us uncomfortable. She was determined to reach the chow.

So often, we make ourselves uncomfortable chasing what we should just leave alone. Our Master knows the path we should follow. His grace really is sufficient.

One never knows what we will encounter on our daily walks. Be wise, be prepared, and always:

Walk by grace!

Is it 9:30 Yet?

The days that Larry and I worked full-time were a stretch for our young, active boxer. One of us would come home at lunch to rescue her from the crate for a short time. That was just the best we could do.

Whoever came home from work first had to deal with Stripezilla. That was usually me. I changed clothes and we headed to the Britt's house. Rocky had also rested most of the day and was ready for action. He was the perfect prescription for Gracie.

Their favorite game was chase. Tug-of-war usually wound up with Rocky lying down and Gracie pulling him around the yard. Rocky was bigger and stronger but Gracie was quick and definitely had more "monkey energy." Face wrestling was sometimes painful to watch, as they bit each other's jowls and faced off with their teeth. We stopped every now and then to check out blood . . . it was generally a small amount on somebody's chin or just inside the mouth.

Matthew was the first of the Britt men to come home. This sent the boxer greeters into action. Gracie and Rocky danced with delight when Matt arrived. On rainy days, the pups would get up on the couch and peer out the window, waiting for Matthew to arrive. Their inner clock told them when he would be pulling in the driveway. As soon as Matt closed the truck door, I released the welcome home committee and Matthew was slathered with boxer kisses. A couple of times they were able to get Matthew to the ground. By the time we rescued him, Matt could barely breathe. They had just about licked the hide off of him.

146

About the time they calmed down, Mike would come home. Round two was equally exciting. Mike always had a rag in his back pocket and it was Rocky's official job to remove the rag as soon as possible and run with it. Gracie had a tongue that just wouldn't stop and Mike had been properly cleaned by her many times. He and Matt were about the only ones who would tolerate it, so Gracie took full advantage of their availability.

Angela and I spent many hours together on the swing, watching the pups and getting to know one another better. Somewhere during this time our families bonded. Angela became Gracie's "other mother" and I became Rocky's second mom. It was a package deal, and Mikey and Matthew became my younger brothers. Charli and later Norma became my sisters-in-law. This somehow made Mike and Angela my parents. This was never really figured out, as they are younger than I am.

After a good hour or so at the Britt's, Gracie had enough of the monkeys worked out of her to come home. After supper, there was more play on the home front. Gracie played all evening every evening, except the days she had spent at day care.

9:30 p.m. seemed to be the "off" button for Gracie. Many times in the evening we would ask the question "Is it 9:30 p.m. yet???" By then, we were ready for bed, too. She would never go upstairs to bed by herself. We were a pack and the pack sleeps together.

Oh, the immeasurable grace of God
That He would give us friends
To share joy
Sorrow
Talents
Time
And a boxer with the grazillas!

The Superheroes

It began as one of our ordinary Saturday morning walks. As I approached Elizabethton High School, I could tell that an event was taking place in the parking lot. Several booths had been set up and people were milling around. Let's go check it out, Gracie.

The event was a fundraiser for the Relay for Life. Many local people had crafts for sale. Local organizations staffed booths, giving information and educating folks concerning their services. Gracie was relaxed and was enjoying meeting and greeting UNTIL she saw THEM. . . .

They were the superheroes. Now Gracie had never seen anything like these critters before and, quite frankly, neither had I. I immediately recognized Super Woman. A pretty blond with red boots, a Super Woman shirt, skirt, and cape, she was definitely Gracie's favorite.

I'm not exactly sure what the other two were. One was dressed in a black, armored suit from head to toe. He had horns or ears. Take your pick. His face was totally covered. The other was even more intimidating. He was huge, had heavy black boots, green legs, a chest full of muscles, scales coming down his arms, black hands which held a club, a large medallion hanging from his neck, and one of the ugliest faces you have ever seen. Oh, I almost forgot, he had wings, too. Now Gracie loves people, but she would have nothing to do with these folks! I finally was able to get this photo, but you will note that I am holding her.

We visited the booths, but Gracie kept a close eye on the invaders. A girl has to know her limits.

Walk softly and carry a big stick!
Make sure Mom is at your side too!

Out of Reach

There are many things in our household that are just for Gracie. Toys, chewies, and bones are provided for her pleasure. There are some things that she chooses to leave alone. For some reason, they simply do not interest her.

But there are numerous items that she desperately wants and is not allowed to have. Take, for example, the shoes I just took off, my cell phone, my hand braces, leather ski gloves, the bag of brand new rawhide chews. Gracie is relentless in her pursuit of these items. When she gets something on her mind, she does NOT forget about it. She doesn't give up until she knows it's out of reach.

We have two safe havens for such articles. The top of Larry's chest of drawers and the top of the refrigerator are the hiding places. She can neither see nor reach these two areas. Of course, it's a little odd to have shoes on top of the refrigerator, but hey, one has to be flexible and sometimes creative in out-foxing a boxer.

There are things in our lives that need to be out of reach. Maybe it's the box of doughnuts or the tray of cookies. Perhaps it's a book or DVD that would cause our minds to dwell outside of the Father's will for us. Such things tempt us to go overboard and do things like eat eight doughnuts or half a box of cookies. The flesh is a powerful force and we all have our weaknesses. Placing those things out of reach protects us from ourselves.

As we resist the devil, he will flee from us!
Sometimes the first step is putting it out of reach!
So
God can bless us with life
And life more abundantly!

It's Officially Time to Get Over It

One of the few rawhide chews tough enough for Gracie is a bully stick. The stick is about twelve inches long and as thick as your index finger. The raunchier it smells, the more it appeals to Gracie.

A new, dried out bully stick smells bad enough to attract any dog. A wet, slimy bully stick is just about unbearable to the human nose. At $3.00, they are well worth the cost on a rainy day when Gracie just can't get enough exercise. You might call it a pacifier. Her powerful jaws can reduce the bully stick to a mere three inches of stink. It is at this point that the bully stick police must be summoned. A three-inch stick is a choking and/or digestion hazard. Gracie's treasure must be surrendered when it reaches this length.

Fortunately Gracie's good nature allows Larry or me to repossess the stick. Just last week, I had to take one away from her. I carefully wrapped it in a paper towel and put it in the sink. There was no way she could reach it there. Her pitiful whines and cries became wearisome. It's time to get over it, Gracie! I moved it to the backside of the basement and shut the door. Down the steps she came and continued the serenade. Perhaps a scratch on the door would help me to understand that she really must have the rest of the treasure. It's REALLY time to get over it.

There seems to be nowhere in our house that is far enough away to put the irresistible object. Finally I had to take it to the outside garbage and roll the garbage can to the road for pickup. It's officially time to get over it, Gracie!

So often we hold on to something that just isn't good for us. The longer we chew on it, the stinkier it gets. Finally, it becomes a hazard. It's time to get over it! It's officially time to get over it! Philippians 3:13–14 says:

Forgetting those things that are behind,
I press toward the mark of the high calling!

Happy Valley

Somehow it's comforting to live in an area called Happy Valley. Three county schools and several businesses bear this name.

Within view of our home is Happy Valley Memorial Park.* It's a lovely cemetery which graces a hillside. Entering the cemetery you will find a waterfall that seems to flow with peace. A lovely plaque on the office door reads, in part:

"Lives are commemorated—deaths are recorded—families are reunited—memories are made tangible—and love is undisguised. This is a cemetery.

The cemetery is a homeland for memorials that are a sustaining source of comfort to the living. A cemetery is a history of people—a perpetual record of yesterday and a quiet today. A cemetery exists because every life is worth loving and remembering—always."

With the permission of the cemetery's owner, Gracie and I occasionally walked there in the early morning hours. Being a responsible pet owner, I was always careful to clean up after my girl.

We quickly got acquainted with the ground crew as they reported to work. Jeff, Mike, John, Austin, Ethan, and a second employee named Mike would often be drinking coffee as they awaited the start of their workday. Gracie knew exactly where to find them and who might have tidbits of their breakfast to share. Somehow she counted them and could tell if one of the men was missing. She looked diligently for the missing person. In the winter she would peer inside the room they congregated in. This usually resulted in an invitation to come in and join the early morning fellowship.

Gracie dispensed her kisses to whoever was up for it. All of the guys were dog lovers and enjoyed her affection. I must say that the ground crew was her favorite. They didn't even mind muddy paw prints.

We soon got to know Gary, Jared, Teresa, Revonda, and Bill as they reported to work. They worked in the office and extended friendship to Gracie and me. To Gracie's delight, occasionally one of them would stop and talk with us.

Gracie loved our walks in the cemetery. A whole new world of sights and smells awaited her there. We were always careful to respect the privacy of anyone who came to grieve. There were times, however, when people wanted to pet her and she brought comfort to a hurting soul. Often folks would open up and share their heart with me while Gracie lavished her love on them. She just had a way of knowing who needed her the most.

I loved walking in the cemetery as much as Gracie did. I found it to be a place of reflection, peace, and prayer. I made it a habit of putting American flags back in place or straightening a flower vase that may have been bumped or knocked out of its holder during the night.

Many of my friends and family were in this place. Larry's parents, aunts, uncles, grandparents, our neighbors, former coworkers, schoolmates, and friends' headstones reminded me of the deposits they had made in our lives.

I was especially thankful for the veterans who had served to purchase freedom for me and for others. I was very interested in reading the headstones and noting how long each person's journey on this earth had been. Some of my favorites were:

"I'm like a fat man in dodge ball, I'm out."

"Love, gentleness, laughter. That was our Mom."

"You gave us a song.
Your warm caring smile,
Your love, joy and truth"

"Say not in grief 'he is no more'
But live in thankfulness that he was"
(on the headstone of a fourteen year old)

"We will play again"

"Jesus will fix it"

"Friend to all"

"In remembrance of the unborn"
I often placed a white rose here, remembering our son, Benjamin.

Reading the headstones caused me to ponder what I might want on my own. Several ideas entered my mind. Deep within my spirit came the answer "If you will write your life upon the lives of others, especially children, your life will continue, as they are living stones."

*Name used by permission

Gracie on a Mission

Carla worked as the children's ministry director at Elizabethton Alliance Church for fifteen years. Gracie and I were invited to present a teaching for one of the Wednesday night "Kids on a Mission" meetings.

Equipped with slides from Gracie's puppydom, toys, her collar, leash, and, of course, Gracie, we were ready to go. Roy kept Gracie upstairs during most of the presentation. Once Gracie came on the scene, I knew I would lose their attention. The main theme of the teaching was learning to walk under authority. One day each of the students would be a person of authority. To become that person, they had to respect the authorities in their lives now. Just as Gracie was in training, so was each one of the children. We talked about ways that I (as Gracie's authority) would set boundaries for her. These rules protected Gracie from harm. Rachel and others had questions. Of course, they wanted to share with me about the pets they had at home.

At the end of the teaching our special guest came down to meet the children. Gracie presented her tricks, which included sit, shake, and saying her prayers. As wiggly as Gracie was, she managed to sit still for each child to stroke her soft fur. Should a little face get too close, that face received some Gracie sugar. Being with children was a special treat for Gracie. Being with Gracie was a treat for the children.

Each student was given a photo of Gracie. The children presented Gracie with a "thank you" bag of goodies, which included a toy that I named "Monkey Lips." Monkey Lips became one of her favorites and always reminded me of Kids on a Mission.

Respect those who have God given authority in your life.
Follow after God and walk close to Him.
Know that you have destiny and purpose.

The Tree Streets
Yard Sale

A section of Johnson City is called the "Tree Streets," as all the streets are named after trees. Each summer, the residents of the Tree Streets have a yard sale. Probably a third to half of the homeowners participate. It's a great tradition filled with food, fellowship, and lots of bargains.

Angela used to be the yard sale queen. When she returned to full time work, she had to relinquish her crown. She is a very efficient yard sale shopper. She very quickly assesses if there is anything of interest to her and then moves on. She purchases very little. I was convinced that her rapid technique caused her to miss things.

In August of 2012, Angela, Mike, Charli, and I attended the Tree Streets yard sale. It was only my second time, so I was still in the learning curve. Angela and Mike found a toy that they purchased for Rocky. It was a battery-operated puppy that not only barked, but walked, too. Rocky was absolutely delighted with the puppy. It was just his speed. The toy soon became handicapped as he roughed it up. It continued to bark. He was mesmerized with it. Rocky was now seven years old and it was good to see him acting like a puppy again.

Treasure the Gift of Today!

Wonderful Wednesday

Rocky and Gracie celebrated their seventh birthday with the number seven pancake and several presents. They had both slowed down a little. . . . Well, actually Rocky had slowed down a lot. Matthew had moved out, having married Norma in June.

One Wednesday evening in August we headed for the Britt's house. We were pleased to find Mike working outside. Rocky and Gracie were so excited. Matthew showed up to help Mike, and the pups went into boxer bolt delight. It was just like old times!

Mike and Angela had decided to ditch the television dish and install an antenna. When I arrived, a rather strange-looking, homemade PVC pipe antenna was lying on the ground. It resembled a cross between a stairway to heaven and Jack's beanstalk. The extra PVC pipe was a wonderful boxer toy. Rocky and Gracie loved the long pieces. Rocky would carry one end and Gracie the other. Beware, human shins, as they may whack you at any time should you interfere with their game. I had not seen Rocky this frisky in some time. I suppose the combination of Matthew, Mike, me, and the new construction sent them overboard.

When the high-rise antenna construction was complete, Mike and I hoisted it from its position on the ground to a standing position. Upright, it now resembled a launching pad. I wondered who would be the first in orbit . . . Gracie, Rocky, or perhaps Angela. She was at work, so she was eliminated from the potential astronaut list.

It was, indeed, a wonderful Wednesday evening. Watching the dogs play with such excitement brought back many memories and made for tired boxers.

What a Difference
a Day Makes

I was in Kingsport visiting my great niece, Kinley, when Angela called and said, "There's something wrong with Rocky. He's just not acting right." I agreed to come by after my visit and check on Rocky. When Gracie and I arrived at the Britt's home, we found that Rocky just did not feel good. He was hiding in small places and had no interest in playing with Gracie. Angela and I agreed that he needed to go see his doctor. She made an appointment for Saturday so she and Mike could go together.

Thursday afternoon Rocky seemed to feel worse. I checked on Rocky again on Friday. His condition had deteriorated.

Larry and I had just gone to bed Friday night when we received a phone call from Charli. Mike, Charli, and Mikey had taken Rocky to the emergency vet clinic. He was a very sick pup. The veterinarian suspected an internal bleed in the area of the spleen. He recommended either immediate surgery or putting him to sleep. Surgery would be very risky, but it seemed to be his only hope.

Mike and Angela talked by phone since she was at work. It all seemed like a bad dream. Just Wednesday Rocky had been happy and frisky, and now he was in critical condition. After much prayer and many tears, they made the decision to put Rocky to sleep. The shock of his illness and death shook us all. Rocky had just turned seven years old. He was in the prime of his life. Boxers are not a long-lived breed, but we had expected to keep him three or four more years.

We put Rocky to rest the next day. Mike built a special wooden box to place him in while Matthew and Mikey dug the grave. He is positioned right next to Bullet (their previous boxer) in the back yard. Headstones mark their graves and a beautiful rose bush grows between them. We gathered around his grave and gave thanks for his life. What a joy he had been to all of us, and we cherish his memory.

Life Without Rocky

I had given thought as to what it would be like when either Rocky or Gracie was gone. The Britts and Howells had blended families because Rocky and Gracie were brother and sister. We were at their house almost every day and had Sunday dinner with them.

We had worked on many projects together, like stacking the eternal piles of wood at the Britt's, building the wood shop, gardening, washing cars, and biking. Many times Mike and Angela came to our rescue. Raising our outdoor building and getting it level had been a project that went above and beyond friendship. Matthew and Mikey had helped with that major project too. Mike had cut several trees down for us and we all had had a part in loading the wood on their truck. Since Mike was Mr. Fix It, there were also some electrical or wood projects he had helped us with.

Angela had blessed us with Sunday dinner each week. She had also sent home leftovers, which had produced another meal for us. She had taught me how to make homemade bread. We had shared recipes and our creative cuisine with each other.

The boys had become younger brothers to me, making Charli my sister-in-law. We had kayaked together, as well as hiked and biked together. Before Matthew had met Norma, we had spent almost every Saturday one summer on the Virginia Creeper Trail riding bikes. He had challenged me to ride to the top of Whitetop, which is seventeen miles up. Although I had not thought I could make it, I had said yes. Much to our surprise, we both made it. Matt lost about fifty pounds that summer. We had become great friends and I am thankful that God knit our hearts together.

I will never forget the day we saw camels, llamas, and donkeys next to the Creeper Trail. The posted sign had said "Camel Rides $5.00." Of course, I'd had to ride one. Matthew Britt had watched as I rode a camel named Matthew! Such fun we'd had together!

I wondered if Rocky's passing would change all this. Were the dogs the glue that held us together? The day after we put Rocky to rest, I asked Angela if she would rather we did not come for Sunday dinner. I thought it might be too painful for their family to have Gracie present without Rocky. Gracefully, she welcomed us to come. Although Rocky was no longer present, we were still family.

When we arrived for Sunday dinner, Gracie noticed that Rocky was not there. She looked around a little, but somehow seemed to understand that he was gone. She quickly settled into her begging routine.

Bear, however, was quite upset that he could not find Rocky. He looked and whined and was very confused when he could not locate Rocky. Rocky's passing seemed to trigger his first seizure. Although he is on medication, he still struggles with them.

It has been almost two years since we lost Rocky. What a special family member he was. He left us with great memories. We still miss his comical ways. He remained Angela's "baby" and everyone's lap dog.

We soon found that the dogs were not the glue that held us together. The Lord had supernaturally drawn us together and we are knit together in His love.

There was one thing that I never did figure out. If Mikey and Matthew were my younger brothers, that would make Angela and Mike my parents. They are both younger than I am. Truly, we were drawn together because our canine kids were brother and sister, but love has kept us together all these years.

> *Now abides faith, hope and love*
> *But the greatest of these is love.*
> I Corinthians 13:13

A Unique Creation

Rocky was, indeed, one of the most laid back, lovable boxers I have ever met. Somehow the couch just did not seem complete without Rocky draped over the back of it. The welcome committee was reduced to Gracie, and then only when we happened to be visiting when Mike or Matthew came home. Matt was married to Norma and lived about fifteen miles away and Rocky was buried next to Bullet.

Although Angela wanted another puppy, she simply was not ready to bring one home. Like us, the Britts were hooked on boxers. Each boxer we have had was a very special individual and we cherish that.

I find it amazing that our Lord creates such variety. He didn't create a flower, He created myriads of flowers, each with a color and fragrance all its own. He spoke the Word and created the heavens, stars, planets, dry ground, plants, animals, and finally fashioned man by His own hand, created in His image.

What glorious variety He designed! With two eyes, one nose, two ears, and one mouth, each of us has our own unique appearance. Our aptitudes, talents, interests, and intellect help define our strengths and weaknesses. With vocal chords that look the same, each of us has a recognizable voice.

Learn to appreciate who you are and were created to be. There is no one exactly like you! You have great destiny and purpose in life. Don't waste a minute lamenting what you are not.

Rocky and Gracie were brother and sister, but they were very different. Angela often called Gracie "turtle head." Being a female, she had a much smaller head than Rocky. She was the dominant one and Rocky freely accepted that. How beautiful is the uniqueness of their creation and how blessed we have been to share life with Rocky and Gracie.

Transition

Gracie actually adjusted to Rocky's absence better than we humans did. Her presence was a link to Rocky and we all appreciated that. She loved getting all the attention and being "everyone's girl." She was beginning to calm down a bit and we noticed that the grazillas rarely took hold of her.

She and Bear had many fun play days. Bear outweighed her by twenty-five pounds, but Gracie was quicker and more nimble. As she aged, we began to notice that after hard exercise with Bear, she would have a sore back leg. X-rays revealed some arthritis in her rear legs, as well as hip dysplasia. It was time to stop the rough and tumble play and chasing with Bear.

Her personality sweetened and she rarely manifested the growly bities. She was content with her place in her human pack and loved to spend time with us. We were both retired now, and it was rare when one of us was not at home. She had become a "Daddy's girl," as Mommy liked to kayak, bicycle, and snow ski. This gave her plenty of time with Daddy.

Gracie was a girl on the go and delighted in our exercise time and visiting trips. She had many people who loved her and looked forward to her daily visits when her friends gave her treats. You just could not help loving a face and personality like Gracie's.

Now eight years old, Gracie was finally growing up. Of course, Larry says I know very little about raising boxers, as mine never seem to grow up. It's true, they are perennial children. This is one of their charms. With a zest for life, love, play, and an indomitable spirit, a boxer is a joy to live with. As one of our veterinarians said, "Boxers are just big goofballs." She had it right.

Forest City, North Carolina

On Sunday morning, January 26, 2014, a litter of boxer puppies was about to be delivered. Although that litter was unplanned by human parents, Rocky and Ginger were expecting their family any moment. Ginger was a petite, dainty boxer, weighing about fifty pounds (before pregnancy), but Daddy Rocky weighed in at ninety pounds, was rugged, and loved to play. Both were fawn colored and had a wonderful home with David and Anna, where they were a vital part of the family. Ginger climbed on her couch, which was located on the screened in porch. This was actually her couch, as she had claimed it some time ago. She loved lying underneath the ceiling fan and lounging.

Rocky was uneasy. He sensed something was going on. He paced and tried to get on the couch to offer his assistance. He was moved so he could see the birth, yet not interfere.

Human parents, Anna and David, were preparing to go to church. Before they left, Ginger delivered two huge baby boxers. She carefully cleaned them and soon after, the new babies began to nurse.

Anna called in "the delivery team," consisting of her son, Rhett Austin, and his friend Brent. As each puppy came forth, Ginger severed the umbilical cord, cleaned the puppy, and then nuzzled it to Brent and Austin for their inspection. They examined each puppy, carefully marked the birth order on paper, and then returned them to Ginger to nurse. Each of the first eight puppies was large and had no problems.

After a four-hour break, the first of two runts was born. Gumball and Lil' Bit needed some special help and were especially babied. They were given extra nourishment and care. What a blessing these puppies were and would become!

We plan, God laughs!

The Call

It was a call that I never saw coming and will never forget. On Friday, January 31 Debbie and I had enjoyed a simply wonderful day skiing at Beech Mountain. The fact that we were now in our sixties did not stop us from enjoying traversing the slopes and the sheer fun of snow skiing. In fact, one of our goals was to live to be seventy and be able to ski for free!

After skiing, we stopped at Fred's mercantile for a little unwind time and a bottle of Cheerwine, a sweet cherry flavored drink. Made only in certain states, there is nothing quite like it. Having fallen asleep at the wheel once while driving home from skiing, I learned that a bottle of Cheerwine was a good investment in health and well-being.

We were in Roan Mountain when the call came to my cell phone. It was Larry. "I need you to come home as soon as possible. I think there is something wrong with Gracie. When I came home from running errands, she just wasn't acting right and did not want to move." I assured him that I would be home as soon as possible. It was now 4:00 p.m. and my expected arrival time was forty-five minutes.

I called Pinecrest Veterinary Clinic to alert them that we might need to come. The earliest we could get there would be around 5:00 p.m. This was their usual closing time. I told them I would assess the situation when I got home and then let them know what our plans were.

When I arrived home, Gracie slowly came to meet me and then just laid down in the yard. Yes, we would be making the trip to her veterinarian, Dr. Karl Kapoor.

I sat in the back seat with Gracie while Larry drove. I helped keep her steady and brought comfort to her. Gracie always wanted her mommy when she was sick. When she was afraid, she went to Larry, but I was definitely her nurse. Arriving at Pinecrest Veterinary Clinic, we opened the door to let her out. A familiar voice said, "Larry? Sue? Is that you?" It was our dear relative and friend, Jan. She was just leaving with her dog. We had not seen Jan in years and were so glad to connect with her again. After a few words, we explained that we had an emergency and needed to get into the clinic quickly. Jan assured us of her prayers and love.

Gracie was able to walk into the clinic slowly. Dr. Kapoor told us she was in shock.

Immediately IV's were begun to stabilize her. What could have happened so quickly?

We had begun seeing Dr. Kapoor when he had graduated from veterinary school. We had been one of his first clients when he had set up his clinic. I had attended his wedding. Now, many years later, his own son was soon to be married. He was an experienced veterinarian, and we knew we could trust Gracie to his care.

Dr. Kapoor explained that he believed Gracie had experienced a tumor rupture, which had caused internal bleeding. She would need to be hospitalized.

It would be a long evening at the Howell household without Gracie. We were shocked that this could happen so quickly. We tried to wrap our minds around what was going on. Dr. Kapoor did his best to prepare us for the worst. It was probably located in her spleen, which was a common site for tumors. The tumor had bled enough to cause shock, but had quit bleeding. Had Larry moved her while the bleed was in progress, she probably would have "bled out," resulting in her death. She was in a critical conditional, and yes, we had done the right thing by bringing her to the vet as an emergency.

We discussed options. The University of Tennessee Veterinary School was two hours away. Dr. Kapoor questioned if she would survive the trip. A local Pet Emergency Center was another option. They had employees that would be there all through the night. But again, that was another move, perhaps a drive of thirty minutes.

We opted to keep her with Dr. Kapoor. By now the superb staff had done everything they could to stabilize Gracie. Dr. Tonya Hinkle was also there. Larry and I asked many questions and looked at various options as we made decisions. Everyone at the clinic treated Gracie and us with the utmost respect, compassion, and love. It was a difficult time and we were dealing with something out of the blue that was threatening the life of our beloved Gracie.

Before we left, we joined hands with the doctors and staff, formed a circle, and prayed for Gracie. We released Gracie to the care of the One who had created her. She was now resting comfortably in her kennel and her vital signs were improving. We left the clinic at about 6:45 p.m. with a lot of information that we wished we didn't need. Dr. Kapoor suspected she had hemangiosarcoma, a cancer of the blood vessels, in her spleen. One can live nicely without a spleen, we reasoned. We were prepared for surgery if we could get her through the weekend. Gracie needed this time to gain strength and get her blood levels up. Amy escorted us to the front door and locked it behind us. We were trying to process this sudden turn of events. Our hope was in God, the giver of life.

Dr. Kapoor called us later that night to give us an update. Gracie's vital signs were improving and he was quite hopeful that she would make it through this crisis. He texted us a picture of Gracie sitting up in her kennel. Her strength was returning and he hoped to be able to do surgery on Monday.

We went to bed that night with heavy hearts. Although there was more room for my feet, the bed seemed empty without Gracie there with us. We were confident that we had made the right decisions concerning her care. We knew she belonged to God and that He had gifted us with her. It was all up to Him. We choose to trust His ability to heal and deliver. And we were able to sleep, resting in His great love for Gracie and us.

We were able to visit Gracie a couple of times on Saturday. She was glad to see us, but was still a very sick little girl. We took her some of her special food (boiled chicken) and she enjoyed a taste of home. Her eating improved. We left plenty for future meals. Blood work confirmed that she was gaining strength.

We were allowed to visit her on Sunday, too. We knew she was feeling better when one of the techs related this story to us. She had opened the door to the kennel area to find Gracie was gone, her IV lying on the floor. Someone had failed to close her kennel tightly. When the clinic cat had approached (thinking she was in control), Gracie had charged out of her kennel and had chased the cat under the cages. That's our girl! She never did like cats, and to think that a clinic cat would get in her face!

Monday morning, as we waited at the clinic, Dr. Kapoor completed the surgery.

He removed her spleen and reported to us that it had several lesions on it, which he believed to be malignant. Specimens would be sent for pathology. We needed to know what we were dealing with so that we could come up with a treatment plan. The surgery had weakened her some, but she still enjoyed our visits.

Oh happy day! After a day or two, we were able to bring our girl home again. It was just not the same without Gracie. We lavished our attention on her as she recuperated. Her meals were meat and broth, and I was with her continually, attending to her every need. We continued to pray for the best pathology report and expected her to make a full recovery. It was so good to have her home again. She seemed to be feeling better and gaining strength each day.

We were surprised to hear that her pathology report was positive for hemangiosarcoma. Dr. Kapoor explained to us that this was about the worst cancer that a dog could have. Hemangiosarcoma is cancer of the blood vessels. He was kind, yet truthful, in saying that he had never had a patient with the disease live for more than six months. That dog was called "the miracle" dog. We asked many questions. We discussed treatment options, including homeopathic ones. We decided to put her on a supplement and consult with the University of Tennessee Oncology Department located in Knoxville, about ninety miles away. We had heard about a new low dose chemotherapy available and we were determined to leave no stone unturned. Dr. Kapoor gave her a steroid shot and this perked her up considerably.

Before we left for our appointment at UT, we were to have a chest x-ray done by Dr. Kapoor. This x-ray showed that the cancer had spread to her lungs in a mere nine days. Our hearts sunk as we felt our Gracie may be leaving us soon.

A snowstorm was in the forecast for our area that afternoon, but we set out for Knoxville, hoping to find some way to treat this vicious disease. We were well cared for by Dr. Cannon and a medical student named Vivek. Tests were performed, information was recorded, a biopsy was done and medications were prescribed. We asked lots of questions. I cannot say enough about the kindness shown to us by Vivek and Dr. Cannon. Although they had known our Gracie for only a short time, they, too, had come to love her and want the best for her.

We decided to do chemotherapy. We needed to wait until Gracie was two weeks post surgery to begin. Today was Friday. We would plan to return on Monday to begin treatments. It was beginning to snow outside and everyone was anxious to leave for the day. We left rather quickly, just ahead of the worst of the storm.

It had been a long, trying day. There were lots of questions we wished we didn't have to ask, much information to process, a long drive ahead, and the pressure of the oncoming snowstorm. We were all glad to arrive at home.

Little Blue Eyes

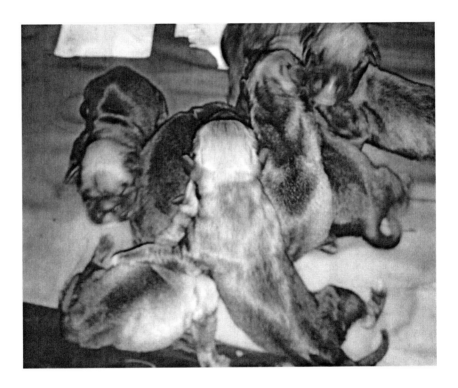

Back in Forest City, North Carolina, Ginger and Rocky's puppies were growing wigglier each day. Little blue eyes popped open and a new world awaited them. Raised in a home filled with love, care, and children, the pups were enjoying all the human attention they were getting. David and Anna's grandchildren, Kinleigh Grace, Emoriee Hope, and Graycin Maddix delighted in the ten little "Indians." The puppies were always glad to see them and curl up on their laps.

There is absolutely nothing like a boxer puppy. The prominent "bump" on their heads makes them look like little cone heads. Their blue eyes sparkle as they attempt to focus on every part of their new world.

Imagine being a new mom with ten babies! Oh my! Ginger may have been a young mother, but she was an excellent one. She kept her babies clean and well fed. The two runts were given extra help by the human family, lest the eight larger puppies wind up with all the nutrition.

Puppy number six was the second one to find her way out of the laundry room and into the kitchen. No doubt, she followed her nose and found where the aroma of food was coming from. She was also the first one to try wet food. Affectionate, yet adventurous, her personality was well balanced.

The Weekend

The decision to do chemotherapy was a difficult one. The cancer had already progressed to at least her lungs and could very well have spread throughout her body. We knew the treatments would be hard on her. The low-dose treatment was no longer an option, as we did not have the time left that was required for it to take effect. The standard treatment would need to be done at the U.T. Veterinary School. We would need to leave her there for the entire day and take her home that evening.

One night, as I took her out to potty, she collapsed on the driveway. I sat with my precious girl, stroking her fur and doing my best to comfort her. Larry noted that we were gone longer than usual. He came outside and carried her into the house. Our hearts sank as we both felt our Gracie slipping away. Once inside, she recuperated and gradually gained strength. We later learned that the collapse had been a sign of another internal bleed. Weakness had caused her to go down, as she was in need of rest.

She collapsed again on Saturday and Sunday. Once the initial collapse had occurred, I knew to watch her very closely so I could let her down gently. She was always at our side and we took great care as she went up and down steps. We placed her on the bed at night and helped her off in the morning.

We continued to look to and trust our Father for Gracie's healing. She was His creation. He had brought her to us and He could handle every aspect of her life and ours. Larry and I both saw we were losing ground in this battle. Only God could help her now. We called the Oncology department of U.T. on Monday morning and told them that we had decided against the chemotherapy. There was no need to put her though that. She was in God's loving hands.

We spent many hours working on jigsaw puzzles just to be on the same level of the house that Gracie was. She generally would lie down underneath the dining room table as we put the pieces together. While pieces of our real life were falling apart, it was therapeutic to be putting something together that made a beautiful picture.

Dr. Kapoor gave her another steroid shot. The second one did not seem to help as much as the first one had. We were all doing our best to make her comfortable and give her a quality life.

Gracie had several visitors during her illness. Carla came and sat on the bed with Gracie. Lovingly stroking her soft fur, Carla had gentle moments of love and affection with our girl. Mike and Angela, Mikey and Charli, Matthew and Norma all came to brighten Gracie's day. She, in turn, brightened theirs.

My friend Debbie came over on a Saturday. She volunteered to go with me so Gracie could go visiting. I needed her with me in case Gracie collapsed. Debbie and I helped Gracie in the car, and Debbie sat in the backseat to steady her. Gracie was subdued as she visited her friends, Judy and Jessica. She was truly glad to see them and accepted their treats and love. We drove to Lowell's house and kept Gracie in the car. By now she was quite tired, but glad to see Lowell. He fed Gracie her favorites as he had been doing for years. Those are precious memories we carry. She was saying her "goodbyes" to those she loved.

Gracie was collapsing every day now. She was visibly weaker. She had someone with her every moment. Our love for Gracie would carry her to the end. She began to lose her appetite and I noticed that she had not had a bowel movement in a day and a half.

I took her out on Monday morning to do her business. She collapsed again. As I sat with her on the grass, I asked Larry to go get the phone. We needed to see Dr. Kapoor for another assessment.

We loaded her up in the car and I sat in the back with Gracie to steady her. Dr. Kapoor came to our car to assess her condition. Everyone at the clinic had been so wonderful and understanding as we had walked through this wilderness. From the front office—consisting of Ann, Danielle, and Ann—to the girls in the back—Tammy, Angie, Jennifer, Penny, Christy, Vanessa, Amy, and Brandy—everyone loved Gracie. Danielle called Gracie "her favorite boxer." Gracie had her well trained. She would stand up on her hind legs and put her front paws on the counter while Danielle gave her "just one more treat."

We had a long history with Ann H. and Tammy. They had worked for Dr. B. many years ago. We had begun taking our dogs to Dr. B. when his children had been in a playpen in the waiting room. Many years had come and gone. Dr. B. was an outstanding veterinarian with a sharp, analytical mind. We trusted our girls to him. Ann and Tammy were just "young pups" themselves!

As Dr. B's patient base grew, he hired a young veterinarian, Dr. Kapoor. Together they established Pinecrest Veterinary Clinic, which was about eight minutes from our house. We were one of Dr. Kapoor's first clients. Although we had tried several other veterinary clinics, we returned to Pinecrest. Their expertise, advanced equipment, and experienced personnel, coupled with a genuine love for animals, made Pinecrest the right choice for this time and season in Gracie's life.

No longer a new veterinarian, Dr. Kapoor was now very experienced. His gentle nature, patience, skill, and knowledge, as well as the atmosphere at the clinic, helped me to know that I had made the right choice in returning to his care. Dr. Tonya Hinkle made a wonderful addition to the team. Dr. Kapoor's wife, Anna, was often at the clinic working on the schedule or books. I had attended their wedding years before. We were all older, a little wiser, and more experienced now. Anna and Karl's children were grown and we all wondered how we had gotten this old so quickly! At our first visit to Dr. Kapoor (after many years of absence) he had said to me "You haven't changed a bit." I told you he was a wise man!

We knew that we were in the best of hands.

The Gift of Kindness

Kindness is a gift we all need to give and receive. Our trip to Pinecrest Veterinary Clinic that morning was filled with kindness. By now, Larry and I had come to the realization that we might have to make the decision that we had prayed we would not have to make. Should we end Gracie's life and spare her continued suffering?

We had stood a constant vigil for three-and-a-half weeks. One of us was always with her, tending to her every need. We had done all we could. We had prayed, we had believed, we had stood upon the Word of God. Our friends had come to our aid visiting, bringing food, praying, and calling to check on us.

At every turn, we received the answer we didn't want to hear. The progression of the cancer was so rapid. In three-and-a-half weeks, we had gone from what we thought was a healthy eight-and-a-half-year-old to an eight-and-a-half-year-old with cancer ravaging her body. We watched daily as she grew weaker.

It was Monday and Mike Britt was off on Mondays. I called Angela Britt to ask if they would be available should we need them. Of course, the answer was yes. They loved our Gracie, too. Angela was Gracie's "other mother." She had grown closer to Gracie since losing Rocky.

Arriving at the clinic, Larry went inside to tell Danielle that we were there. Very shortly Dr. Kapoor and Angela, his assistant, arrived with a needle, expecting, I suppose, to give Gracie another steroid shot. Karl and Angela spoke with us at great length about the situation. Gracie had not eaten in a day and a half, nor had she had a bowel movement. We had concerns that the cancer had spread to her digestive system.

We discussed all options. Larry and I had many questions, which Karl patiently answered. I looked deeply into her eyes and, for the first time, saw a plea for help. Because of our great love for her, I knew what we must do. It was time to say goodbye to our beloved Gracie. All too soon, her time had come to an end.

Karl asked us if we would like to bring her inside the clinic, or would we prefer that he come to the car. Always thinking of Gracie, I asked him to come to the car. I would be with her until the end. Karl and Angela went inside the clinic to retrieve the items they would need while Larry and I said our goodbyes to our doghter. Our hearts were ripped apart knowing we were losing her.

Karl prepared me for what he was about to do. I had been at the side of every one of our dogs that has had to be put to sleep. It has been the final act of kindness that I can do. I would have it no other way.

Larry walked around the building as Karl and Angela approached the car. We all handle things in our own way and we bless one another with kindness when we respect that fact.

Fortunately, we didn't realize when we pulled out of the driveway that it would be the last time Gracie would ride with us. Going places had been such a joy to her. Somehow, not knowing made it easier for us. God is so merciful to show us only what we need to know. We only need to take one step at a time and follow His lead.

Gently, lovingly, and with the greatest of kindness and respect, Karl and Angela assisted Gracie as she took leave of us. Gracie gradually laid down in my arms as she left us and came to a peaceful rest. No more suffering, no more pain, no more collapsing, weakness, or difficulties. Her beautiful eyes no longer pleaded with me for help. She was at rest. She had made it to the other side. And we had been left behind.

Larry came back to the car. At least two of us were in tears—maybe four of us. I cannot say, as tears washed my eyes and soul. Karl extended the greatest of kindness to us and was fully supportive of our decision. He put his arm around Larry and assured him that he had done all he could. Indeed, we did have that satisfaction, but we no longer had Gracie. She had returned to her Creator, Who had blessed us with her for over eight years.

I called Mike and Angela to confirm that we would need them. Ginger, Mindy, Heidi, and Gina Marie were all buried close to our home and Gracie would be no different. We had already decided on the place. She would be laid to rest just beyond the carport steps in the backyard. As with Heidi and Gina Marie, a beautiful rosebush would be planted at her grave to remind us of the life she had shared with us.

We left Gracie in the back of the car. Mike and Angela arrived to help us with the grim task of burying our beloved boxer. With four of us digging, we made good progress in spite of the tears. Occasionally, I would stop digging, go to the car, lay my head on Gracie, and cry. My time to touch her was coming to an end. How many times had I stroked her velvet fur and held her in my arms?

Mike had offered a week or so before to build her a casket, but I had told him I preferred to wrap her in her quilts and blankets. I went inside and choose a couple of her favorite toys to be buried with her. Her "Beauty and the Beast" quilt would be wrapped around her. How appropriate, how fitting, for surely she fit that description. Gracie had several little stuffed hearts that she had often brought to us. One was tiger striped (as she was). Another was bright green and said "you R great" on it. Somehow, she had brought that to us at just the right time. My favorite was a tiny red velvet heart. So soft and precious. I kept this and to this day, it's on my dresser.

Having completed our digging, we wrapped her in the soft quilt and added another one of her blankets and a few toys. Together, we gently lowered her body and our hearts into the earth. I laid on the ground, half inside the grave and half in the yard and cried until it seemed there were no tears left. Larry, Mike, and Angela joined the tearful farewell. Respectfully, they gave me all the time I needed to say goodbye.

Drained of emotion, I was finally able to release her. I arose and we began the painful task of covering her body. Each shovel full of dirt said goodbye and widened the distance between us. Never again, on this side of eternity, would we touch her. Her time had come and gone.

We completed the burial and mounded the dirt to allow for settling. I placed a flower on the grave. Years before, Carla had given me a kit to make a concrete square stone with Gracie's name on it. Complete with her paw prints, the stone was marked "Elizabeth Grace" and was laid to rest. It had been Larry's idea to use it as a headstone.

We thanked the Britts for their love and kindness. No one could understand like they could. Rocky and Gracie's time on this earth seemed all too short, yet ours must go on. We were all exhausted emotionally. With hugs and tears, we bid them farewell and began life without our Gracie.

Because it was February, I had to wait until spring to plant the rose bush. Each week I would purchase a fresh rose and put it on her grave. When the rose withered, I removed the petals and sprinkled them on her grave. She continued to bring color and life, even in death.

The burial was six months ago. The tears flowed freely as I recounted this chapter in Gracie's life. She will always be a part of us. God richly blessed us through her.

Kindness goes a long way and will never be forgotten. Dr. Karl Kapoor, the staff at Pinecrest, Mike and Angela, and our friends and family rallied around us as we endured our loss and began a new era in our lives.

"If there are no dogs in heaven, then I want to go where they are."
— Mark Twain

"God will prepare everything for our perfect happiness in heaven, and if it takes my dog being there, I believe, he'll be there."
— Billy Graham

"The dog is the most faithful of animals and would be much esteemed were it not so common. Our Lord God has made His greatest gift the commonest."
— Martin Luther

"Be comforted, little dog, thou too, in the Resurrection shall have a tail of gold."
— Martin Luther

Picking up the Pieces

It's never easy to lose a family member, especially one you lived with. You expect to see them at any moment and their presence is greatly missed. Life will never be the same without Gracie. She gave so much, loved so many, and enriched our lives immeasurably. She had a face that just would not quit.

Our family and friends were so supportive of us during this time of grieving. We were showered with cards, flowers, hugs, prayers, and many phone calls. Tears washed our hearts and cleansed our emotions.

I avoided walking in all of our regular places. It was just too hard to go back to the places that she and I had frequented. During my first walk without Gracie, two people asked me where she was. Everyone had loved Gracie and they were used to seeing us together.

I was thankful for the time we'd had with Gracie. Eight-and-a-half years didn't seem like enough but that was what she was given. I focused on the positive things. She had not suffered long, and we had done everything we could to make her life rich, full, and happy. Her life here with us had come and gone ever so quickly. She was in a better place and was still greatly loved.

Elizabeth Grace
August 22, 2005–February 24, 2014

We shall always remember Elizabeth Grace
The sunshine girl with her radiant face.
Such energy and a zest for today
Her spunk, her spirit and love for play
She showered us with joy each day.

From her early days as a little pup
She turned our world downside up.
She challenged our wills right from the start
So much to our lives she did impart
She is forever sealed within our hearts.

Elizabeth means consecrated to God
A life as bright as goldenrod.
Grace is unmerited favor and love
Sent to us from our Father above
She illuminated our lives with His great love.

With a stripe like a skunk on her precious forehead
"One magnificent piece" an admirer said.
White socks on her feet; always happy, never blue
Her faithful heart so pure and so true
Swirling fur on her neck with an attitude!

With heavy hearts and eyes filled with tears
We remember our gift of eight and a half years
He gave her to us as a beautiful treasure
And the love she gave was without measure
Sharing life with her was a delight and pleasure.

To each of you who prayed and cared for her
Who fed her treats or stroked her velvet fur
We thank you for loving our dear little one
And shared with us her joy and the fun
Her memory will shine as bright as the sun.

This poem hangs in the Oncology Department of the University of Tennessee Veterinary School at their request.

What's Next, Lord?

As the weeks passed, we discussed whether or not to get another dog. Except for short periods between dogs, we had always had one. Without a dog, our home seemed empty. Yes, dogs require time and are a financial commitment, and yes, we were now in our sixties, but the Howell household needed a dog.

We discussed other breeds. By now, we were so hooked on boxers that I questioned if I would be disappointed with another breed. We knew boxers and we knew we loved everything about them. Okay, so maybe we could do without the flatulence and tolerate a little less activity. Their shorter life span and tendency toward cancer and heart disease were things to be considered, but not a deal breaker.

Angela and I took walks and talked about our next boxers. We discussed names, color, and the fun we would have being puppy moms together again. We planned to purchase from the same litter. She would want a male and we would get a female. We began to get the word out that we were looking.

Larry and I wanted a fawn-colored boxer. Since Gracie was brindle, fawn would be a nice change. I had a plan in my head to find a litter locally that had just been born. I would be able to see them shortly after birth, visit regularly, and choose which one I wanted. This would give us about three months between dogs. It was a great plan and I began the search.

About a month after losing Gracie, the search became serious. I connected with a woman in North Carolina who seemed to fit into "the plan." Her female had just given birth to three puppies. She was looking for the best of homes and preferred to sell her puppies to someone who had already raised a boxer. We talked one Friday and everything seemed to gel. She was excited about placing one of her pups with me. She emailed me their photos and told me that I could come and pick mine out at any time. I would wait until the pup was eight weeks old before I would pick it up.

Later that evening, she texted me and said that with all due respect to me, she did not feel like one of her puppies was the right choice for me. I was confused and wondered what had changed her mind. Letting go of that possibility, I continued my search via computer.

Finding Gracie had been so easy. It had just happened, even before I had known we would need another puppy. I knew the Lord had provided Gracie for us. This was different. There seemed to be no clear direction.

I found some adorable pups in Knoxville, but I returned to an ad that had been listed on Sunday for boxer puppies in Forest City, North Carolina. Five puppies were listed, one male and four females. Angela had responded on Sunday and was informed that the male had already been adopted. I emailed about the ad on Sunday evening and did not get a response. In fact, a total of three hundred people responded to this listing.

On Friday, I mentioned to Larry that I had emailed about the puppies, but had not heard back. He offered to send a second email. "What can it hurt?" I reasoned. Within minutes I received a phone call. "I'm calling you about the boxer puppy" Anna said. I had responded to so many ads that I had to ask her which one. "The puppies in Forest City," was her reply.

There was an immediate connection between Anna and me. I relayed to her our recent loss and our long history with boxers.

This divinely inspired conversation had His fingerprints all over it. She had one female left. I asked her to email me a photo of the puppy and one of each of the parents, Ginger and Rocky. The puppy was absolutely adorable. With a prominent intelligence bump, gentle eyes, black mask, and a few little white toes, she was just what we were looking for.

Anna and David were going to deliver one of the other puppies to Morgan and Ricky, who lived in Canton. The meeting place was Hendersonville, North Carolina, which was a little over an hour's drive for us. Anna offered to bring the available puppy along so we could see her. I appreciated this offer so much. I also told Anna that should she find a home for the puppy tonight, I would understand. "No," Anna said. "You have first choice."

Were we ready for another puppy? Larry and I discussed it thoroughly. He was the one who said, "I think you need to at least go look at the puppy." He was right. She was exactly what we were looking for. We made plans to go see her. We rarely carried cash, but that night we were able to pool our resources and come up with $250, the asking price for the puppy. I dug out a soft, lilac blanket just in case we brought her home.

Saturday morning was a cold, dreary day. A light drizzle fell from the sky. We began our journey not knowing what the day would bring. How would we react? Was it too soon to bring another puppy into our home? I knew in my spirit that we would know the right thing to do when the time came. We drove on, trusting that the Lord knew the answer and that He would direct our hearts.

Just outside of Erwin, Tennessee, we saw a beautiful rainbow. I knew we were on the right track. A rainbow is the reminder of God's promises.

We arrived in Hendersonville and found the restaurant we were scheduled to meet at. We located David and Anna. Anna had both puppies wrapped up in blankets. She presented the smaller, darker one to me.

Oh, my goodness! She was absolutely beautiful! It had been a long time since I had held a baby boxer. Her sweet, gentle personality melted my heart and I simply could not get enough of her. Morgan and Ricky arrived to pick up their new family member. Her name was Dixie and she got to meet her new big brother, Max. Max was also a boxer. He had lost his sister nine weeks before. Actually, his sister had passed away the very day Dixie was born. Max was gentle and loving toward the new puppy.

While the puppy moms held the babies, we got to know each other. We also asked David and Anna many questions about the puppies. As

Morgan watched me cuddle the puppy, she turned to Larry and said, "I think it's a done deal." To which Larry replied, "I think it was a done deal when we pulled out of the driveway."

Yep, he was right. Puppy number six of Rocky and Ginger's litter was soon to become ours. I was overjoyed and in awe of God's goodness to us. She was born on Sunday of the week we had found out Gracie was sick. She had been prepared for us!

Not wanting to wipe out all of our cash, I asked Anna if they would take a check. To my surprise, she said yes. I opened my checkbook and found a rainbow on the check. Anna, David, and I knew we had made a divine connection. Three hundred emails were sent responding to the ad about the puppies and now, a week later, the last available puppy was delivered into our hands.

Amidst goodbye hugs and puppy kisses, we said our goodbyes. The little Tar Heel (the nickname of the University of North Carolina) was soon to become a Tennessee Volunteer. Her black heels and pads remind us of her state of origin. Larry drove and I cuddled our new family member.

We discussed names. Larry suggested Abigail. "Doesn't Abba mean father?" he asked. As a matter of fact it does! She looked like an Abby. On the drive home, we decided on her name. Days later we added her second name, "Rose."

Fashioned by her Father's Hand
Abigail Rose
Abigail means Father's joy or gives joy
Is welcomed into the home and hearts of
Larry and Susan Howell
On March 29, 2014

Born: January 26, 2014
Weighing 9 pounds on March 29, 2014

God is good all the time
And all the time
God is good!

Tabitha Grace Britt
Born to Matthew and Norma
on October 23, 2014
weighing 5 pounds and 7 ounces
and 19 and a 1/2 inches long

Grace Abounds!!!

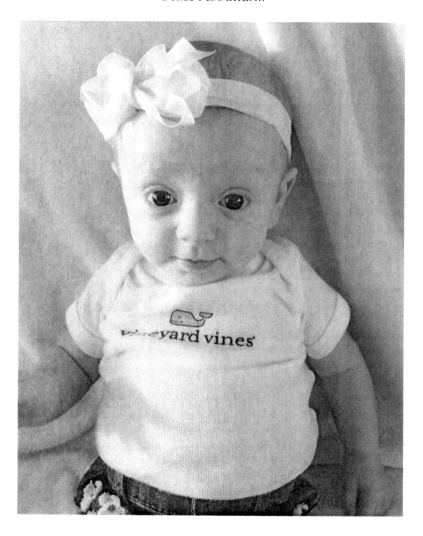

About the Author

Following a dream and possessing a mere two hundred and forty dollars, Susan Miles moved from her hometown of Waukegan, Illinois to Upper East Tennessee. The following day, in June 1968, she met her pen pal of four years. That September, they were married.

Susan Miles Howell has written poetry, puppet scripts, children's books and children's teaching series. Her first published book was *The Father's Heart*. Her creativity has included handmade crafts, designing and creating worship banners, tie dying, silk painting and refurbishing baskets. Susan's heart is displayed through worshipful dance and instructing future generations in expressive praise and worship. She has also worked in the medical field and served as a Children's Pastor. An avid snow skier, kayaker and bicyclist, Susan enjoys God's magnificent creation. She and her husband, Larry, along with their boxer puppy, Abigail Rose, reside near Johnson City, Tennessee.

ɔformation can be obtained at www.ICGtesting.com
ˋ USA
)10715
/00001B/1/P